MURDER IN THE YOGA STORE

The True Story of the Lululemon Killing

PETER ROSS RANGE

Hawthorne Press

Washington, D. C.

For Linda

CONTENTS

Chapter One

DISCOVERY

Friday night

T he first blow must have struck Jayna Murray so hard in the back of her head that she couldn't gather her senses to fight back. Muscular and exceedingly fit, Jayna often did handstands and cartwheels for fun at Lululemon Athletica in Bethesda, Maryland, the yoga apparel boutique where she worked. In exuberant moments, she swept colleagues off their feet and spun them around. She was training for a marathon.

Around Lululemon, Jayna was known as the strong one, the woman with the beaming smile and can-do attitude who could handle the heavy boxes and would tackle anything. Anything, that is, except the assault that ended her young and promising life in a hail of blows and blood. Anything except an explosion of rage that remains a mystery to this day.

Saturday morning

Rachel Oertli arrived, coffee in hand, just before 8 o'clock on Saturday morning at *her* shop, *her* boutique, *her* beloved Lululemon. The Bethesda store that Rachel managed is part of a Canadian chain that sells expensive "yoga-inspired" sportswear, the kind that stretches where you need to stretch, clings where clinging looks good, and makes you feel righteous just walking around. But Lululemon is also a high-concept purveyor of a way of life. It's a shrine of upscale sweat. With its innovative "technical" clothing mainly for women, Lululemon sells healthy living for healthy profits. The shop is replete with inspirational slogans, like: "This is not your practice life. This is all there is." And: "Jealousy works the opposite way you want it to." The cheerful exhortations adorn Lululemon's signature red shopping bags and some of its apparel. "Sweat once a day," for instance, was printed inside the cap that was found to contain the blood and DNA of the murderer.

And on this morning, as Rachel made the short walk from her well-appointed apartment across the street—she had timed her commute at 28 seconds—she was keenly aware of how perfectly Lululemon fit into this low-rise block of Bethesda, Maryland, an affluent suburb of Washington, D.C. With chic shops and new restaurants, the once dowdy street had been transformed by the real estate planners from drab and downscale to trendy and pricey—and rebranded "Bethesda Row." An airy shop with natural wood flooring and an open-beam ceiling, Lululemon blended just fine with the Petra boutique (Sonia Rykiel dresses at $1,500), the posh Bluemercury salon and spa (fusion facial for $175) and the tiny but crowded Georgetown Cupcake shop (Red Velvet at $2.75), everyone's favorite high-calorie indulgence. A busy Barnes & Noble bookstore anchored one end of the block, a gleaming Mercedes-Benz showroom the other. Bright spring fashions already filled the display windows above hand-laid brick sidewalks.

Rachel ran Lululemon with a strong hand. Dark-haired and dark-eyed, an outgoing woman with an instinct for retail, she was a no-nonsense manager, a stickler for cleanliness and order. That morning, Rachel couldn't believe it when she found the store's front door unlocked. She swore to herself, upset that Jayna, who was in charge of closing up the night before, must have forgotten to lock up. Even though Jayna was one of her best friends—Jayna sometimes stayed over at her apartment—Rachel didn't like this kind of carelessness.

Right away, Rachel knew that something was off. A table had been moved, mannequins had fallen over, a flat screen TV had crashed to the floor, and there—right there!—garments were scattered all around. Walking around the table, Rachel saw blood on the floor—bloody footprints. Rachel thought she heard a low moaning coming from the back. She froze, then hurried toward the door.

Rachel burst out onto the sidewalk. It was a cool but pleasant pre-spring morning, March 12, 2011. It promised to be a good sales day in Bethesda, and not only for Lululemon. Right next door, the shiny new Apple Store, bristling with the high-tech toys of our time, projected the slick salesmanship of Steve Jobs into the willing arms of Bethesdans with cash. Only the day before, Apple had released the new iPad 2 to runaway sales. This morning the true believers were already gathering for the store's 10 o'clock opening.

Sitting before Rachel as she rushed from Lululemon was a young man on a bench, drinking coffee and smoking a cigarette, waiting to score his new iPad 2.

"Is everything okay?" asked Ryan Haugh. "Do you want me to go in with you and take a look?" Her voice quavering, Rachel said yes.

Rachel stopped halfway into the shop. Scared and breathing hard, she let Ryan go ahead. He saw bloody sneaker prints running helter-skelter, mostly toward the back. He worked his way past the clothing racks with their $108 yoga pants, $58 sports bras and $68 T-shirts. He passed the changing rooms and bathrooms, walking right past the flat-screen TV. "Anybody here?" he yelled. No answer.

Ryan saw a half-open door with a large chalkboard. It read: "May each of us equally enjoy happiness and the root of happiness." Pushing on another door, he found that it was blocked—by a human being. Or rather, a human body.

The body lay in wide smears of blood. Assuming the body was that of a man, Ryan reached down and pushed on it. No reaction.

Ryan turned to leave the store in a hurry. As he passed the bathrooms, he saw someone else lying on the floor: a woman. She was surrounded by debris and blood spatter, and had been cut with something sharp. There were lacerations on her hands, arms, upper chest and an especially big one on her forehead, a wide gash that had dripped in a rivulet across her face. She was also bound hand and foot with plastic zip ties, her arms awkwardly positioned on the floor above her head.

Her eyes were closed but her chest was moving; she was alive. Ryan flinched when he noticed that her black yoga pants had been ripped open at the crotch.

Rushing outside, Ryan told Rachel that a man lay dead in the store but that someone inside was still alive. "She's been sexually assaulted," he said. Rachel called 911: "I'm a little crazy right now....I am so scared that one of my girls is hurt. Oh, my God! Oh, my God!"

It was worse than she thought.

Within minutes, Montgomery County Police Officer Christin Knuth roared up in her patrol car. Telling Rachel and Ryan to stay outside, Knuth drew her Glock .40mm handgun and entered Lululemon. She hugged the right side of the shop near the clothing racks, her pistol in firing position. "Anyone here?" she shouted. "Show yourself!" Knuth assumed that "there's likely someone in this store who is going to jump out and either try to hurt me or try to kill me."

As she moved deeper into the store, the officer saw the bound woman lying in the bathroom. She forced open the door to the rear hallway, stepping into the shocking scene: dried blood everywhere, walls blood-spattered up to six feet high, a red smudge on the rear exit door. Before Knuth, facing toward a wall, lay the body.

Knuth saw that it was not a man's body but a woman's. The victim lay face down in a crimson swamp, her blond hair a mass of reddened tangles. A tool box had fallen across her shoulder and neck, its contents spilling out. The black-and-yellow soles of her running shoes faced up, but the toes pointed down. She could almost have been taking a nap.

Officer Knuth saw that the woman's pants and underwear had been neatly slit between her legs, exposing her buttocks. She leaned over to touch the woman's neck, feeling for life.

"I felt nothing. There was no pulse. She was cold. She was stiff."

Outside, Rachel was sitting in a police cruiser, barely controlling her emotions, telling an officer what she knew. Life suddenly felt upside down. She wondered what could have gone wrong.

And: "Who is dead?"

Chapter Two

JAYNA MISSING

At River Place, a sprawling apartment complex in Arlington, Virginia, Marisa Connaughton was becoming increasingly upset. Where was Jayna? Why hadn't she come home last night? Her cat had not even been fed. Jayna never missed feeding Hobo.

Marisa and Jayna were best friends, like sisters, really, though so many people called Jayna their best friend that it was hard to keep count. Marisa and Jayna lived on different floors of River Place, but they had keys to each other's apartment and saw each other every day. They texted and worked out and ate meals together. They shared everything, boosting each other's confidence in their relationships, their work, their careers.

Jayna, at 30, was a force to be reckoned with. Many people said she was the most dynamic person they had ever known, a fun-lover and risk-taker, and, most of all, a positive influence in their lives. "Jayna was different," said Leah McFail, who also considered Jayna her best friend after they spent four months together on a ship in a college Semester-At-Sea program. Loud, bubbly and possessed of a "cackling whole-body laugh," as Leah put it, Jayna was known as the life of any party, the spark in a relationship, the woman who stood on principle and called out her friends when they stepped over certain lines. She was also an adventurer, physically and spiritually. Jayna would rock-climb or go spelunking or try trampolining and trapezing or seek out the hard stuff during her frequent world travels, like visiting Mother Teresa's orphanage while in India.

For her thirtieth birthday just a few months earlier, Jayna had gone bungee-jumping. She'd already been sky-diving, so leaping off a bridge into the 191-foot Columbia River Gorge in Oregon was a natural next step. With several friends watching—and one shooting a video—Jayna plunged through space, arms spread like a fledgling eagle, aiming for the swirling water below. Her scream of delight pierced the frigid air of the valley like a bell's peal. She then posted the whole thing on YouTube. The four-minute video with Tom Petty's haunting music—"I'm learning to fly but I ain't got wings / Coming down is the hardest thing"—would become her ode to life, a closing frame for her goodbye smile.

It was that smile that everyone talked about. People said Jayna lit up every room. She was once called a California golden girl, though she never lived in the Golden State. "Jayna brought the fun," said her friend, Patrick Byrnett. "You noticed Jayna when she walked into the room," said Judd Borakove, owner of CrossFit, a Bethesda fitness center where Jayna trained.

Even though she worked in a high-end women's clothing boutique, Jayna flat-out admitted that she had no fashion sense. Jayna let her friends tell her how to dress and often borrowed their clothes. "She was still wearing T-shirts from high school," laughed Marisa. Still, Jayna was one of the belles of the ball, in a purple satin dress, at the wedding of her friend, Cynthia Isaacson, in Minnesota only months earlier. "She wants to visit every continent before she dies!" announced the emcee at the wedding dinner, not knowing that she'd already visited all but one, and that she would never make it to the last: Antarctica.

Everybody had Jayna stories. Matt Deschner told how Jayna led the way up the Pyrenees Mountains when she was in the freshman class at Saint Louis University in Madrid, Spain. Her sister-in-law, Kate Murray, chuckled about Jayna's "goofy" faces and ability to make people laugh with an over-enunciated sing-song voice. Courtney Kelly, a close friend who worked at Lululemon, said Jayna was honest and blunt, but not to a fault. "She called you on your shit without being offensive." Melissa Jersey, a friend in Houston, recalled Jayna's amazing ability to get other people to do silly things, like mooning the security camera of Melissa's next-door neighbor, then celebrating with backflips.

Those backflips! Those cartwheels! Those handstands! Jayna's mother, Phyllis Murray, had to stop little Jayna from cartwheeling down super-market aisles, even when they lived in Australia in her youth. Phyllis cleared furniture out of the living room to give the budding gymnast space. Trailing after her two athletic older brothers—"she did everything we did," said Hugh Murray, her oldest brother—Jayna seized sporting challenges by the throat. At age 11, she followed her brothers on a 150-mile bicycle ride to benefit the National Multiple Sclerosis Society. She played football with the neighborhood boys and "they knew she could take it," said Dirk Murray, her second-oldest brother. A high school coach saw her spinning one day and recruited her to throw discus and shot put; she began to set high school records.

And, finally, there was dance. Jayna was a natural dancer, all lithe muscle, strength and grace. Starting at an early age, she was a standout in her classes. But with her athletic build, "she didn't have the right body for ballet," recalls her teacher, Michelle Smith, of the Houston Met in Texas. Since "she was phenomenal at tap," however, Jayna was recruited to dance with Savion Glover, the New York sensation who succeeded Gregory Hines as America's tapping master. After many clinics and performances in New York, Los Angeles, Chicago, Washington and Houston, where she grew up, Jayna was planning a professional life on Broadway—until an older dancer explained to her what a cruel and short-lived career it could be. Jayna opted instead for an international education in business and communications, graduating from George Washington University in Washington, D.C. in 2003.

Jayna went to work in marketing at Halliburton, the international oil field services company based in

Houston. But after six years, she wanted more. Jayna enrolled in grad school at Johns Hopkins University in Washington. She decided to earn not just one master's degree, but two: one in business administration, the other in communications. By the time of the attack at Lululemon, Jayna was only ten weeks away from finishing both degrees.

While at Johns Hopkins, Jayna's course had taken a critical turn: Lululemon came into her life. It began when Marisa arrived home one day with a bright red tote bag emblazoned with slogans for a healthy, eco-friendly and fulfilling life. They were just the kind that Jayna liked: "Do one thing a day that scares you." "Creativity is maximized when you are living in the moment." "What you do to the earth you do to yourself."

The red bag was Lululemon's manifesto for righteous living: 37 sayings to "guide our culture," as the company so confidently put it. The aphorisms appealed to the health-conscious environmentalist and idealist in Jayna, the young woman who once considered earning a law degree because she was appalled at reports of human trafficking and child sex abuse. Jayna was immediately intrigued by Lululemon's manifesto and she began to study the company for her business administration courses. She liked its philosophy—combining high-end garments with high-minded ideals. She also liked the way it supported staffers' personal, professional and fitness goals. Encouraged by one of her professors, Jayna got a job at Lululemon, adapting her schedule to her coursework at Johns Hopkins.

Jayna's life, work and academic paths were now intertwined at the yoga store in Bethesda. She took the free Sunday morning yoga classes at the store, she used the company's free passes to fitness clubs, she helped develop the store's social media outreach. Jayna became a believer in the product, a dyed-in-the-Kool-Aid member of the sisterhood of Lulu girls, as the mostly under-30 staff called themselves in the special camaraderie of a female-run store. Almost all were college-educated, some with law degrees or master's degrees, but they were passionate about the retail brand and Lululemon's approach to a work-life balance. "I couldn't believe I was being paid to go work out," laughed one Lulu girl when she started.

At Johns Hopkins, Jayna decided to write her master's thesis on Lululemon. For a communications course, Jayna wrote a media plan for the Canadian company—recommending that Lululemon's founder and its new CEO take special media training in New York. She also wrote, with tragic prescience, a "Crisis Communication Plan" that Lululemon could implement in case of an in-store disaster.

For all her tight relationships and the high esteem in which her friends held her, Jayna was, of course, only human. She enjoyed staying up late watching junk television like *The Biggest Loser* and drinking cheap Barefoot wine with Marisa. "I'm intoxicated, tired and want to go to sleep," she texted a friend one night. On a Valentine's Day, one of her friends thought it odd to see Jayna crying because Fraser Bocell, her boyfriend in

Seattle, had sent her flowers instead of what she had requested—money for books. "She wasn't perfect," laughed the friend.

Jayna's high-energy personality made her a chronic nail biter. "Are her nails gone?" asked Jayna's mother nervously when the police were trying to identify the dead woman in the yoga store. Jayna's bluff style, her natural exuberance, could sometimes make her a little too bossy for some people, though she was just as often admired for an engaging frankness. In the end, however, her candor may have been a liability, a trigger in a volatile situation with a crazed person bent on destruction.

Yet in spring 2011, Jayna was in a very good place. After she received her master's degrees in May, she planned to drive across country to Seattle to be with Fraser, the man she'd known since seventh grade and now hoped to marry. She also hoped to join Lululemon's top management team at the Vancouver headquarters, only a two-and-a-half hour drive from Seattle. Jayna was "extremely happy," said Marisa.

But on this Saturday morning, Marisa knew that something must be wrong. Jayna was supposed to meet Marisa on a corner near River Place as she finished an early-morning, four-mile footrace. Marisa arrived and looked for Jayna. A statuesque and striking blond, five feet, five inches tall and 160 pounds, Jayna with her million-watt smile was always easy to find in a crowd.

But there was no Jayna.

Chapter Three

THE ATTACK

In Bethesda, the bloodied woman on Lululemon's bathroom floor moaned as a police officer sliced the zip ties off her wrists and ankles. Within minutes, she was in a nearby hospital. She told the nurses her name was Brittany Norwood. She was 28.

Brittany was a small woman, five feet, two or three inches tall and 123 pounds. Toned and fit, she looked like the former soccer player she was, just right for a sales person at a high-end yoga-wear shop. "She was petite but jacked," said a Lululemon colleague, recalling how Brittany once won an impromptu push-up contest with a customer in the store.

A star athlete in high school outside Seattle, and a stand-out scholarship soccer player at Stony Brook University on Long Island, Brittany was "very fast, tough and hard-tackling," remembered one of her coaches. Often the only African American on her teams, Brittany nonetheless fit in seamlessly with her teammates. Now she liked working out, doing yoga, taking fitness classes. Brittany, in many ways, was like Jayna. Both women had grown up in exceptionally close-knit families in middle-class suburbia. While Jayna had two brothers, however, Brittany had a huge family: four brothers and four sisters, nine kids in all, eleven people in the family. Brittany's family, like Jayna's, stressed achievement, family values and strong religious beliefs. Brittany's mother, like Jayna's, embraced a Bible-based Christianity and made sure her daughter attended church. Like Jayna, Brittany made good grades and participated in school activities, such as a club devoted to marketing, budgeting and professionalism skills. She even ran her own babysitting service.

At Lululemon, Brittany embraced the company ethos of self-improvement, especially since it seemed to help sell the clothes. Brittany was considered a good sales person, or "educator," as Lululemon labels its sellers. She fit right in with the other free-spirited young women (and a few guys) who made up the sales staff. One photo—the only picture that includes both Brittany and Jayna—shows a couple dozen happy folks in front of Lululemon's store in Georgetown, one of Washington's busiest shopping districts. They are cheering the 2010 Marine Corps Marathon. Several of the girls are waving signs at the runners, such as: "Why do all the cute ones run away?" And: "Don't stop (that's what she said)." Brittany's sign read: "You have great stamina—call me!"

Brittany was always laughing and smiling, mostly interested in having a good time. She liked living well and looking good. Her hair was always just so, her clothes looked sharp, she picked the best items to eat, drink and buy. Maker's Mark was her bourbon, Marc Jacobs was her clutch bag and the best desserts were her choice at dinner, said her friend, Eila Rab, a Lululemon sales person who was also close to Jayna.

While other Lululemon employees, especially Jayna, loved the raucous atmosphere and Mexican spirit at Uncle Julio's, the eatery right next to the Apple Store in Bethesda, Brittany sometimes preferred to drink sake at Raku, an Asian fusion restaurant around the corner. She liked going to McCormick & Schmick's, the pricey seafood restaurant in Bethesda, and to Sequoia, an imposing waterfront eatery on the Potomac River in Georgetown.

"She claimed to be a big foodie and knew all the hot spots," recalled Eila, who held a Master's of Business Administration from Vanderbilt University. Eila was struck by Brittany's expensive tastes and wondered how she could afford them on Lululemon's $12-per-hour wages. Eila was also impressed by the care and detail with which Brittany furnished her apartment. With its nearly all-white décor, it looked almost like a showroom. Brittany's closet was the most amazing thing to Eila. It resembled a wall in a boutique, primarily filled with Lululemon clothing. "It looked like a store display," said Eila. "I've never seen a neater closet in my life."

"I'm a neat freak," admitted Brittany.

While Brittany had been at the Bethesda Lululemon for only a month, she was already trying to make a big change in her life. She knew that her brothers and sisters were doing well—two were engineers, one was a doctor. Yet Brittany was "still just going through the motions," said her brother, Chris Norwood. He told her it was time to find a career, not just a job. Brittany had complained that it was impossible to make a living selling stretchy pants at a yoga store. The other Lululemon girls laughed when they heard that: Of course, what did she think? No one was there to make money. It was a stepping stone to something else.

The something else for Brittany was personal training. A friend, Nora Mann, had left Lululemon and become a personal trainer at Equinox, a luxury gym just around the corner. She was making good money, she said, and urged Brittany to apply for a slot that had opened up at the gym. Brittany emailed her résumé and had her first interview just two days before the attack. She had been invited back for a second interview. "We will be reaching out to you soon to set this up!" an Equinox manager had written in an email.

But now Brittany lay in a hospital bed, wounded and in shock. She was a mess. In addition to the cuts on her face, chest and arms, she had a nasty slice in the web between her thumb and forefinger. The gash across her forehead was caked dry, a thick knot of blood had settled beside her nose. Her cheeks were cross-hatched with fine cuts.

The Montgomery County Police Department had gone into full emergency mode. Besides the cops at the yoga store, another was sent to the hospital to find out what had happened to Brittany. Detective Deana Mackie, a 19-year veteran cop who specialized in homicide and sex crimes, sat down beside Brittany's bed. Gently, she asked Brittany to recount everything she could remember about the attack.

Over the next 45 minutes, Brittany poured out a chilling story of events on the previous night that took the detective's breath away. Brittany painted a picture of brutality, verbal abuse and sexual assault. Even when working in the worst parts of Montgomery County—the neighborhoods not as prosperous as Bethesda, with their sometimes violent mix of newcomers and gangs—Detective Mackie had never come across a narrative as sordid as Brittany's.

She and Jayna had closed up and left Lululemon at 9:45 p.m., said Brittany. Jayna headed for her car, Brittany for the Metro subway. But a few minutes later, Brittany discovered she had forgotten her wallet, which contained her Metro farecard. She had called Jayna to ask if they could return to the store; Jayna had the keys. Once they were inside, the women searched for 10 minutes but couldn't find Brittany's wallet. Jayna offered Brittany her own Metro farecard so she could get home that night.

What happened next was the fulfillment of every woman's worst fears about nighttime assault. As the two young women started for the front door, said Brittany, two men suddenly jumped them. The men were dressed head to toe in black, their faces covered by masks. The sneak attack began with one man slugging Jayna in the back of her head, said Brittany, now choking on her words. Another man sprang out from behind a clothing rack and hit Brittany in the head, dragged her around by her hair and cut her with a sharp object all over her body.

"He had me by the hair, told me if I said another word he would slit my throat," she sobbed.

It was a darkening nightmare: two men in the full surge of aggression, bent on hurting and taking, brimming with misogynistic anger and spewing racist insults: *you dirty bitch, you dirty whore, you dirty nigger*. Brittany's head was spinning; at times she felt that she couldn't even see, she said. It was hard to keep track of the mayhem and the destruction, the moment-to-moment shocks, the sense of worse things to come. She talked as if she were in some kind of horror film, tied to a script she could not control.

The nastiness led exactly where Brittany sensed it was going. One of the attackers pushed her down in a bathroom, its floor strewn with broken glass. Telling the detective about it, Brittany's voice broke again. Mackie softly urged her on. "This is very difficult for you. ...You're doing a great job," she said.

Words began tumbling out of Brittany's mouth: "I was still trying to fight him and tried to get up and he hit me across the head, I just fell back and hit my head on the ground, he pushed me back...he had a knife of some kind...he told me if I didn't shut up and stop moving he'd make sure I'd never have kids...and was cutting me down my stomach...and he said something along the lines of 'being with a dirty nigger, I've never been with one of these,' and he was cutting my pants and he was gonna rape me."

Even as he prepared to assault her, said Brittany, her attacker took perverse delight in abusing her. "I don't fuck with dirty niggers," he said. "You're so dirty, I wouldn't even use my dick to rape you."

But then he did.

After quickly raping her with his penis, said Brittany, the man turned sadistic. He grabbed a wooden clothes hanger with serrated edges, one of dozens in the clothing store, and inserted it repeatedly into Brittany's vagina. The assault seemed to go on forever, she said. "He told me he wouldn't stop until I actually came."

Brittany and Jayna were both screaming—in vain. During the relentless sexual assault, Brittany said she could hear sounds from the adjacent Apple Store—signs of life, maybe salvation! She thought Apple staffers must be cheering over their iPad sales. Brittany tried to fight with her attacker. He told her to shut up and be still. Then he demanded that Brittany show him how to open the cash registers and safes.

While Brittany struggled in the bathroom, the other man was assaulting Jayna. "Jayna kept yelling and fighting, and he just kept hitting her," said Brittany. "I think he dragged her to the bathroom and she was still trying to fight with him but then I just heard something break. ...He was just repeatedly hitting her and she was just screaming and yelling and I couldn't do anything...I don't know if she was able to stand up, I don't know if she was on her knees or what...He was dragging her by the hair."

The attacker then pulled Jayna into the rear hallway. He beat her for so long and so hard, said Brittany, that her screams for help gradually faded into faintness, then nothing.

Now Brittany was crying in the hospital, her words to Detective Mackie coming in a crescendo of sobs. She said she had tried to aid Jayna, then to escape out the back door, but she was jerked back by her hair. In the rear hallway near the exit, all Brittany saw was blood, lots of blood around Jayna—more blood than she'd ever seen before. She said it to the detective five, six times. She kept coming back to the blood. "There was so much blood! I remember trying to help her. I tried to help Jayna. ...She was bleeding so much!"

Brittany was crying so hard her speech was almost unintelligible. Finally, she forced out the words: "She was so *innocent*!"

Brittany was breaking down, blaming herself for not assisting Jayna, for causing the problem in the first place by forgetting her wallet. "I just want to cry," she said.

"You can't even think that it was your fault," responded Mackie. "You [could not] know what would happen."

But there was one startling thing in Brittany's story: She didn't understand that Jayna's fading screams had ended for a reason. Jayna was dead. Brittany didn't know it.

"Can you tell me how my friend is doing?" she had asked Mackie when the detective arrived. Mackie dodged the question—she didn't know how Jayna was, she said, because she had not yet been to the Lululemon store. She had come directly to the hospital.

Several times, Detective Mackie asked Brittany to describe her attackers. Brittany replied that one was "really tall," over six feet. The other was quite short, barely taller than Brittany. Both were of medium build.

"How about their race?" asked the detective. "Could you tell?"

"I have no idea," said Brittany. The men were wearing gloves and ski masks so tight that she could not even see skin around their eyes. Her attacker had her by the hair most of the time and was behind her. When he'd first raped her, it had happened so fast she had not seen his penis.

"Could you tell by their voice?" asked the detective.

"By their voice I would say maybe white."

In the end, Brittany's attacker had bound her hands and feet with plastic zip ties and left her on the bathroom floor. After that, she said, she blacked out. When police had found her the next morning, she lay semi-conscious on her back, hands tied together and her arms stretched above her head.

Chapter Four

BETHESDA BREAKS LOOSE

I n Bethesda, all hell was breaking loose. Bethesda Avenue had become a media circus, jammed with police cars and TV trucks, their microwave towers waving at the sky. Yellow police tape stretched across the sidewalk, holding back the gawkers. A police officer covered Lululemon's show windows with brown paper, blocking the grisly view.

Among the cops and prosecutors converging on Bethesda was John McCarthy, the state's attorney. Red-haired and athletic, a feisty man of Irish descent, McCarthy ran the 100-person Montgomery County prosecutorial corps. McCarthy was known for his courtroom oratory, his skill at prosecuting hard cases, and his hands-on involvement in his work. "I knew this was going to be a *red ball*," he said—a hot case with a lot of public attention.

McCarthy immediately called assistant state's attorney Marybeth Ayres to join him. A lithe blond woman with a fondness for fitness, Ayres was a lawyer's lawyer, an uncompromising prosecutor with sharp recall of investigative details and a special interest in criminal personalities.

When they arrived at the store, McCarthy and Ayres found a trove of forensic evidence: bloody footprints from large men's shoes and small women's shoes; a broken vase and scattered flowers in the bathroom where Brittany had been attacked; box cutters that must have been used to cut her. Just outside the bathroom, they saw the wooden clothes hanger used to rape her. On the floor in front of the dressing rooms lay Brittany's bag, where she said she had dropped it. The prosecutors also saw clumps of blond hair on the spot where Brittany said Jayna had been violently dragged by the hair towards the back room. The mayhem suggested a titanic battle.

The police department had already assigned the case to two lead detectives, Jim Drewry and Dimitry Ruvin. The two men were a well-matched pair of opposites. Drewry, 61, was the oldest and most respected member of the detective corps, with 23 years in homicide. Tall, down-to-earth and affable, Drewry was known for his dapper sweater vests and a trust-inducing style that got hardened killers to spill their guts. The Lululemon homicide would be his last active murder case before retirement.

Ruvin, 31, was the youngest member of the twelve-person homicide and sex-crimes squad. He had only three years in the elite unit after eight years as a patrolman and station detective. Quick and youthful, Ruvin favored a neat goatee and wide-knotted ties. The son of Russian immigrants who settled in Baltimore when he was 15, the young detective spoke perfect English with an easy charm. Ruvin saw Drewry as his mentor—"he's a legend"—but on this case, Ruvin sometimes got out front.

Drewry and Ruvin were seasoned cops, but they were appalled by the scene. It was an episode of *CSI* come to life. "Everything was there, right where Brittany had said it was," remembered Ruvin. Worst of all was Jayna's body, lying where Brittany had said Jayna's screams had ended.

The forensics people were already mapping the space, taking pictures, bagging key items. Blood spatter on the walls. A broken cell phone near the rear door. Red handprints on the wall where the TV had fallen to the floor, then another handprint on the emergency push bar at the rear exit. There was even a rope around Jayna's neck that matched a coil of rope on the shelf above her head. In the store's back room they found Jayna's laptop computer and a wallet lying in plain sight on a chair. A bottle of red wine—Jayna's favorite—had rolled under the chair.

Drewry hadn't been counting on something this gory for his last active homicide case. "I sure got a doozy," he said.

There was something unearthly about the store, remembers Ayres. She entered Lululemon on Saturday night to review the scene, and found it unnerving: "They had this weird, dim overhead lighting. The store was quiet. There were mannequins and racks of clothes and it was almost like in a movie, like someone could jump out from anywhere. It was really creepy."

Word spread quickly in Bethesda that two women had been attacked in the Lululemon store. Both had been raped, one had been murdered. The cash registers and safes had been emptied. The gruesome attack was the work of two masked men in black. "It was like an electric shock," recalls Rollie Flynn, who was in line at Bethesda Bagels, only 100 feet from Lululemon, when the cops began closing off Bethesda Avenue. The story sounded like a crazy robbery gone wrong, a Hollywood horror flick. It also seemed impossible for it to happen in a place like Bethesda, right on Bethesda Row, one of the charmed spots in prosperous Northwest Washington and its suburbs.

Women, especially, were suddenly on their guard, hostage to a new feeling of vulnerability. "I thought, 'Suppose this could happen to me?'" recalls Flynn, who became more wary when arriving home at night. At J. McLaughlin, a fashionable women's clothing boutique across the street from Lululemon, a manager told a reporter she might issue panic bracelets to her staffers, and would no longer allow anyone to work alone in the shop. Just up the street, the young staff at Georgetown Cupcake worried about their safety. They identified with the Lululemon girls, whom they saw all the time.

State's Attorney McCarthy got a call from a friend whose daughter worked at the little pastry store. "John, tell me there are not really two madmen running around Bethesda doing this stuff to women," she said. "My daughter was in Georgetown Cupcake until 10 p.m. last night, closing out the store exactly when the murder occurred."

McCarthy replied: "I can't tell you that, because that's exactly what we're hearing."

It was not only the brutality of the crimes that unnerved the community. It was the crossing of the invisible line that divided the sometimes coarse and chaotic world of Washington, especially its crime-prone eastern districts, from the protected and distant planet of suburbia, like Bethesda and its neighbor, Chevy Chase.

Greater Washington leads a double life. The city's elite exists in a charmed realm of affluence and shared values. Seventy-nine percent of Bethesda residents have college degrees and an astonishing 50 percent hold graduate or professional degrees. Harvard is a household word around the capital. The region is eco-conscious and health-minded. Bethesda on weekends becomes a fishbowl of bright colors as well-Spandexed bicyclists flash past.

Bethesda's placid streets always carry a sense of stability and security, freedom from fear, and a certain lightness of living. Any given day on Bethesda Row sees a mix of the serious and the silly, of the sporting life and the working life, all worn easily by people who feel comfortable in their space. The prevailing style is shabby chic, where you can't tell the millionaires from the garden-variety upper middle-class folks. Sockless Guccis and a deep winter tan are the mark of Palm Beach, and stand out like a sore thumb in Bethesda. The whole place has more the feel of Martha's Vineyard on a nice summer day.

"It's a community of achievers," says Seth Goldman, whose $90-million company, Honest Tea (now owned by Coca-Cola), is just up the street from Lululemon. "It's what you've done, not what you've made, that counts."

Time once called this high-achieving world "the bubble on the Potomac." Those in the bubble are shielded from the dysfunction around it. Bethesda has a very low crime rate. A handful of robberies and burglaries, a few car break-ins, and some teen-age shenanigans are more common than crimes of violence. Jayna's murder was one of only two in 2011. There was only one in 2012. "They call us when there's a dog in the road in Bethesda," laughed one police official.

But now there was mayhem in the middle of town. With Jayna's murder and Brittany's rape, the cocoon of suburban bliss was pierced, the social contract broken. The criminals were not staying home; they were coming to the innocents. "It was an attack on a way of life," said Roger Berliner, Bethesda's representative on the powerful Montgomery County Council, the governing body of Maryland's richest county. "Something like this goes to your core."

"People were thinking: Circle the wagons!" said Jane Fairweather, a Bethesda real estate agent.

The anxiety that flooded the collective psyche drove an outpouring of citizen leads to the police department's public tip line—more than 300 in a few days. Some may have also been motivated by the $136,000 in announced reward money—--$125,000 of it coming from Lululemon's billionaire founder, Chip Wilson.

Some tips reflected the fevered churnings of a frightened populace. One suggested that Jayna's murder was not a robbery gone wrong but a contract killing gone wrong. The hit men's victim was not supposed to be Jayna but a different woman who had swapped shifts on Friday night with Jayna, said the tipster. He had one thing right: Jayna had indeed swapped shifts. But she had exchanged shifts with her friend, Mikell Belser, not with the woman named by the tipster.

Some tips were based on nothing more detailed than a sighting of a tall man and a short man at a McDonald's ten miles away. Another mentioned two guys "suspiciously" parked near a 7-Eleven store 35 miles away in Manassas, Virginia. A psychic had a vision of a "heavy set male who did not have a lot of hair" accompanied by a "tall thin male" going into Lululemon. One store owner reported a tall man acting strangely. One woman reported a short man acting strangely in a pick-up truck. Another noted two young men wearing hoodies in front of a nearby Italian deli.

But one thing many tips had in common: they referred not to "two masked men in black," but to "two black men." Nowhere in the news reports had it been claimed that "two black men" perpetrated the attack. The police had even noted in a press release that the race of the attackers was unknown. But in the popular imagination, "two men in black" quickly and seamlessly mutated into the bugaboo of the 'burbs, "two black men."

The tip line had become a Rorschach of the community. Residents used it to project their expectations and fears, including an underlying racial element, onto the new mayhem in their midst. The frightening reputation of the eastern precincts of Washington provided a model for the madness. Even though Bethesda is a decidedly liberal political community—Montgomery County gave President Obama 68 percent of its vote in 2012—the tip line opened a window on unspoken racial fears in the nearly all-white bubble.

Chapter Five

AUTOPSY

The shock of Brittany's story—murder, rape and brutality by two marauding men—was still reverberating throughout the community when the next blow fell. It was known at first only to a handful, like Detective Ruvin and the state's medical examiner. But when it circulated more widely, people were shocked and disbelieving. It was the autopsy of Jayna Murray.

Jayna's body had been taken to Baltimore for a post-mortem by a Maryland state medical examiner, Dr. Mary Ripple. A forensic pathologist, Ripple had done more than three thousand such autopsies. But as she examined Jayna's body, Ripple realized she was seeing something she'd never seen before: a person killed by several hundred bludgeons, cuts, stabs and even rope wounds.

As she began keeping track in her medical notes and making photographs, Ripple was astonished at the numbers: 232 blunt force injuries and 99 sharp force injuries. Jayna had more than 100 wounds to her head, 39 of them on her face, which was defiled like a Jack-o'-lantern. The top of her skull was cracked in eight places.

Her neck and chin were bruised by a rough rope. There were even contusions on her legs.

On the back of Jayna's head the medical examiner found 37 wounds, a whole separate battlefield. Finally, there was a deep gouge on the lower right of Jayna's skull, a three-and-a-half-inch stab directly into the cerebellum of her brain. This was the wound, concluded Ripple, that killed Jayna.

In all, there were 331 separately identifiable wounds on Jayna's body (this was a conservative count; some of the wounds were overlaid and could not be counted as separate blows). Dr. Ripple's autopsy report ran to 26 single-spaced pages and 37 photographs.

Jayna's wounds told the story. First, she had fought long and hard to save her life. Dr. Ripple had identified 105 of her wounds as defensive: blows to the hands and forearms that come from a person's efforts to fend off an attacker. This meant a prolonged struggle between a determined assailant and a tenacious defender.

Even more striking and shocking: Jayna must have lived through the first 330 cuts, slices, bludgeons and stabs. Only the 331st—the knife thrust to her brain—ended her life. All the other wounds showed bleeding or bruising that could only occur when a person had blood pressure from a heart that was still beating, said Ripple.

To inflict 331 blows would take time—and effort. During the trial seven months later, the judge sat at home one night and banged his fist down 331 times. He said it took him eight minutes. The prosecutor calculated that if one allowed three seconds for each blow, it would take 16 minutes. But Jayna's killing probably took longer: The murderer had to move around the store to pick up new weapons.

From the nature of the injuries, and from the blood found on the tools and implements scattered about the store, it was clear that Jayna had been attacked by at least five and possibly as many as ten different weapons. They included a hammer, a wrench, a straight-edged box cutter, a wheeled box cutter, a metal peg used to hold up mannequins, a steel rod called a merchandise peg for hanging clothes, perhaps a razor and, finally, the rope. The fatal stab probably came from the long serrated knife that the Lululemon girls used to trim fresh flowers for the sales floor. The knife usually hung over the sink in the back room, 15 feet and two doors away from where Jayna was found dead. The murderer must have been exhausted—a sweating, frenzied attacker, a person gone mad.

Chapter Six

HEARING THE MURDER

If Lululemon was a fashionable gateway to yogic serenity, the adjoining Apple Store was the opposite: a slick conduit to permanent connectivity. One company was created to channel and calm the senses, the other to bombard them. Lululemon was muted and pastel; Apple was gleaming and white, framed in chrome.

The Apple Store was the liveliest enterprise on Bethesda Avenue. Seen at night from the shop-filled arcade across the street, Apple rose like a phoenix, its bitten-apple logo a hanging moon. With its forward-edge technology—iPads, iPhones, MacBooks—the store had in a year's time become the block's commercial magnet. On this Saturday morning, despite the police hubbub and rumors of mayhem, Apple was overflowing, with a line on the sidewalk. People still wanted their toys.

Like everybody else, the cops were drawn to Apple, but for different reasons. The store shared a wall with Lululemon; it was bustling all the time; it had a large staff of sales people and technical advisors. Apple was also a security-conscious operation—no surprise, given the expensive baubles on offer. Apple had indoor and outdoor security cameras, while Lululemon had none. Apple also had security guards.

Apple's outdoor surveillance camera overlooked the store's rear entrance beside a parking lot, right next to Lululemon's rear entrance. This was a lucky find. Even if Lululemon had no video of its own, maybe something— or someone—had passed through the Apple camera's field of view.

Cueing up Apple's video, investigators at first saw nothing of interest—a few pedestrians coming and going to their cars. Tedious and frustrating, the video at first looked like just another dead end. Then suddenly, right on the screen, two men walked past the rear of the Apple Store, coming from the direction of Lululemon. Dressed in black, the men were moving swiftly. One wore a black knit cap, the kind that can be pulled down to make a mask. He was also carrying a black backpack. Could these be the attackers? The scene fit perfectly with Brittany's story. It occurred almost exactly one hour after Brittany said she and Jayna had reentered Lululemon.

For Detectives Drewry and Ruvin, the surveillance video was a crucial break. Now their task was to locate the two men in black. The only problem with the video was that the two men's faces could not be seen very well.

Then another piece of sensational news: Two Apple staffers said they had actually *heard* the attack as it was happening.

After 10 p.m., said an Apple manager named Jana Svrzo, she and the other managers were tallying up the day's receipts. She began hearing unusual sounds through the east wall of the Apple Store where iPad and iPhone accessories hung. It was the wall that Apple shared with Lululemon.

As she approached the wall, Jana heard a strange combination of thuds, screams, and agonized breathing. "It sounded like something heavy was being hit or dragged," she remembered. "Some grunting, some thudding, some kind of high-pitched squealing, yelping. ...A female voice, like hysterical sounds."

Unnerved, Jana hurried upstairs to get Ricardo Rios, her senior manager. "I don't think I'm crazy, can you come down and listen to this?"

Jana and Ricardo returned to the accessories wall. Ricardo leaned forward. He, too, heard a hysterical female voice. Then he made out heavy panting "like when you can't breathe, you're trying to catch your breath and talk." Jana said it sounded like a deep *unhh*!—a forced expelling of breath.

Finally, between the yelps and the thuds, they both heard two female voices, one to their right, one to their left.

The voice on the right said, "Talk to me! Tell me what's going on! Why won't you tell me? Talk to me!"

The voice on the left, more hysterical, said: "Stop, oh God! Please help me, God!"

Things began to slow down. "For a little while afterwards, there was still some grunting, a few screams or yells, but no conversation, no words," said Jana. All she heard now was a kind of desperate panting, what an expert later called "agonal breathing," the tortured air-sucking that occurs in the throes of death.

Jana and Ricardo walked away from the wall. Later asked what he thought was going on, Ricardo said he regarded the noise coming through the wall as just "some drama."

The two Apple staffers had just heard the sounds of Jayna Murray's demise. Apple's indoor surveillance video shows they first noticed the noises at 10:10 p.m. and stopped hearing anything at 10:19 p.m. They had nine minutes to react in some way to what was happening in Lululemon. Unsure and reluctant to interfere, unable to conceive what was occurring next door but also unwilling to investigate, they had opted to do nothing. They had not done the easy and obvious thing—call 911—though they were in a store full of phones. They hadn't asked one of Apple's two security guards to bang on Lululemon's doors to see if everything was okay. They had shirked simple civic responsibility, turned their backs and returned to counting Apple's money.

Chapter Seven

HOT SUSPECT

To find the two men in black, Detectives Drewry and Ruvin began asking other stores for surveillance videos, tips, anything unusual that they may have noticed on Friday or Saturday. At first, they came up dry. In Bethesda, most merchants don't feel the need for security cameras, especially outdoor ones. But in his fourth or fifth store, Ruvin unexpectedly hit pay dirt. At a popular hardware and house wares emporium next to the booming Mercedes-Benz dealership, a manager had noticed something unusual on the morning of the crime. It involved Kevin Lowery (not his real name), a neighborhood hang-about who was regarded as a bit of a local nuisance.

On Friday, the day of the murder, said the hardware store manager, he had noticed Kevin, who is African American, walking towards Lululemon with two white men. The store manager had never seen him walking around with two white men before. And something else: Kevin was carrying a black backpack.

He'd seen the man wandering around many times before, but never with a backpack.

All Ruvin's bells went off. One of the men seen walking past the Apple Store in the security video had been wearing a black backpack. Brittany had reported that her attackers sounded like white men. Kevin was walking with two white guys. Even if Kevin himself had not been an attacker, he could have been a lookout, standing outside—a common ploy in store robberies. This looked hot. The detectives now had a real, live suspect.

Ruvin began investigating Kevin. Kevin was known to spend time at the bar of a restaurant one block away from Lululemon. He was sometimes belligerent and aggressive, especially towards women. A manager at the restaurant told police that Kevin once said he "wanted to fuck [the manager's] daughters." Kevin normally showed up every day, said the manager, but he had not come in on Friday, the night of the murder, or on Saturday, the day afterwards. Suspicious, Ruvin queried police headquarters—what do we have on Kevin? It turned out the man had a long rap sheet, including assault with a gun, reckless endangerment and a host of other charges. An old warrant was still outstanding for Kevin's arrest for furnishing alcohol to a minor.

Ruvin then learned that Kevin was being treated in a local hospital for bloody wounds to his head. The hospital was in Takoma Park, Maryland, eight miles away. How did Kevin get bloodied? Why would he go so far away for treatment? If you had nothing to hide, you would go to Bethesda's Suburban Hospital, only a mile-and-a-half away, practically walking distance. It was the hospital where Brittany was treated.

Clues were fitting together. Kevin could have been injured in the Lululemon scuffle. With the arrest warrant in hand, the police on Sunday night went to the hospital in Takoma Park. Kevin was holding an icepack over a swollen eye when the officers walked in. But Kevin had his story ready. He said he was bloodied because he'd been assaulted on Saturday night in a club by a man wearing dreadlocks. The assailant was always hanging around a social service agency in Bethesda and robbed people on the streets, said Kevin. The man with the dreadlocks also hung out a lot with another ne'er-do-well, a short Hispanic man, said Kevin. The Hispanic man was homeless and wanted for murder, Kevin claimed. Warming to his story, Kevin even insisted that he had been across the street from Lululemon and seen the two men attack a woman in the store.

This was wild stuff. Kevin was proving to be an elusive suspect, a great source or a very imaginative storyteller. Drewry already harbored doubts that Kevin was one of the Lululemon attackers. The detective was known for his ability to sense a person's deceptions, dissembling, discomfort—and guilt. His feel for personalities and behavior gave him a great touch during interrogations. But something about Kevin told Drewry they were going down a cold trail. "I'm not feeling this guy," Drewry told prosecutor McCarthy.

By Monday the level of panic in Bethesda was palpable. Police Chief J. Thomas Manger decided it was time to hold a press conference to reassure the public that the cops were on the case. In mid-afternoon, he stood before television cameras in front of Lululemon, now adorned with flowers, mementos and signs mourning Jayna and Brittany. "Two beautiful souls, one lost, one deeply hurt," read a note. Manger said that both women had been raped and that the police had some "good solid leads." They believed that the attackers had entered the store through the unlocked front door just seconds after the two women had returned. He announced a search for the men described by Brittany, and enlisted the help of the entire community.

The manhunt was on.

Chapter Eight

BRITTANY AND THE SNEAKERS

Detectives Drewry and Ruvin still had not met Brittany, the only living victim of the attacks. After one day in the hospital, Brittany had gone home to the Washington, D.C., townhouse she shared with her sister, Marissa Norwood. On Monday night, the detectives made the long drive from Montgomery County police headquarters to the townhouse, located in a neighborhood near Howard University, the crown jewel of historically black colleges in America. Brittany occupied the basement apartment while her sister lived in the upper two floors. When Drewry and Ruvin arrived, Brittany's parents were there—they had flown in from Seattle. At least two of her brothers were there, too.

Drewry, as he almost always did, led the conversation. With his close-cropped graying hair and sweater vests, Jimmy—as the other detectives called him—could always set a casual and relaxed tone. Particularly with Brittany, a young woman in her late twenties, the detective—who was African American—struck a fatherly note.

Brittany retold the story of the attack. Still a wounded person, she spoke softly, adding details that she hadn't mentioned before. Her attacker, she said, was wearing a hoodie over his ski mask. His voice sounded like he was in his mid-twenties—and he smelled of cigarettes. The men were definitely white, she thought, and were laughing a lot during the attack, acting as if they were playing a game.

"It seemed like a video game where they steal cars," said Brittany.

"Grand Theft Auto?" asked Ruvin.

"That's it," said Brittany.

There were other astonishing details. When she tried to escape out Lululemon's back door, her attacker grabbed her and shoved her down atop Jayna's body, into her blood. The attacker told her that what she and Jayna were going through was all Brittany's fault. "This is because of you," he shouted as he pushed Brittany onto Jayna. The only reason Brittany wasn't in the same spot and in the same condition as Jayna, he said, was that Brittany "was more fun to fuck."

Hearing Brittany's story, with its sobs and wrenching details, was painful for the detectives. "She was crying, she was shaking—it was hard listening to her," said Ruvin. "I'm thinking, 'I can't believe what she went through.'"

A new detail had come in from the forensics search of the Lululemon store. A detective, Sergeant Craig

Wittenberger, had discovered a pair of large men's sneakers stashed on a rack in the store. "Wow!" said Wittenberger, holding one sneaker down to the floor. Its sole tread perfectly matched one set of bloody footprints that tracked around the store. The attackers must have, for some reason, left a pair of sneakers behind. But there was one odd thing: The shoes had blood on their tops, but the soles were clean; they contained no blood. They also had no laces. "Wow!" he said again.

Ruvin asked Brittany about the men's shoes. Because Lululemon offered a small selection of men's workout wear, these sneakers were for men to wear while measuring for alterations, said Brittany. The shoes belonged to the store. Startled, Ruvin made a mental note that the shoes had not come from the outside on the feet of one of the bad guys.

Then Brittany offered another revelation: The attackers knew her name and where she lived. She said one of the men must have dug into her bag on the floor, which contained bills from her cable company and gas company. They knew exactly where to find her.

As they left Brittany's apartment, the detectives realized they had gotten more than they bargained for. Driving north towards police headquarters, Ruvin was mulling everything over. He couldn't stop thinking about the large men's sneakers. By telling the detectives that the shoes belonged to the Lululemon store, not to some intruder who had left them behind, Brittany had changed their significance. That single fact had the younger detective's wheels turning.

Chapter Nine

LULULEMON WORLD

The Lululemon world had lurched into full damage control mode. Christine Day, Lululemon's CEO, had flown into Washington. In a moment of crisis, Day became the face of the company.

Lululemon was one of the roaring retail success stories of the 2000s. A niche seller of expensive yoga wear mainly for women, the company had in a decade gone from a single beachfront shop in Vancouver to nearly 200 stores with annual sales of $1 billion. The business was the brainchild of Chip Wilson, a former surfer and snowboarder. Wilson was a free-spirited Canadian who discovered yoga at middle age, and decided to make and sell specialized women's wear for the rapidly growing exercise movement.

A gifted trend-spotter, Wilson hit the sweet spot between pricey fashion and a cultish commitment to self-improvement. Wilson became one of yoga's Pied Pipers, or at least the man who dressed the followers of the real gurus. Borrowing from the libertarian-conservative writer Ayn Rand, Wilson hoped to "elevate the world from mediocrity to greatness." Wilson's genius was to combine marketing with a devotion to fitness and environmentalism. He seized on the burgeoning wellness business and helped reframe yoga from an eccentric cult of hyper-stretched spiritualists to a trendy movement of body-conscious young women and upscale moms.

His strategy worked. "When I'm wearing Lululemon stuff, I take myself more seriously as a runner. It makes me want to work out," says one lawyer-mom.

When CEO Day arrived in Washington, she granted all Bethesda store staffers time off and organized group therapy sessions at a nearby hotel. To some, these were a comfort; to others they were somber gatherings that only intensified their disorientation, grief and fear.

Many of the Lululemon girls were, quite simply, in a state of terror. They, like the rest of Bethesda, were convinced that two ruthless killers were on the loose in their midst. Gena've Ramirez, another Lululemon staffer who was also Marisa Connaughton's roommate, was frozen with fear that the attackers might somehow find her. "I was alone [after Jayna's body was discovered]. Suppose they knew where Jayna lived and were coming to do something!" she said. Courtney Kelly, even though she had family nearby, remembers sitting in her car, terrified to walk from the street to her sister's front door in the evening. "When I got there, my hand was shaking so hard I couldn't get the key in the door."

Eila, the Lululemon girl who was Brittany's friend, was so distraught that she and her boyfriend departed for a week in Shenandoah, the bucolic Virginia valley 70 miles to the west.

Christine Day's first concern was assuaging the pain of the Murray family. She ordered a plane to pick them up in Houston on Monday. In Washington, Day organized a dinner for the Murrays and all 100 of Lululemon's employees in the area's five Lululemon stores—a group hug giving everyone mutual support.

In a gripping irony, Day seemed to be following some elements of the "Crisis Communication Plan" that Jayna had written for Lululemon at Johns Hopkins University. One of the first lines in Jayna's paper was: "Human life is most important." Jayna had focused on the dangers of sexual assault at Lululemon because most of the chain's staffers were women. "Many of the employees wear Lululemon apparel while working," she wrote. "To put it plainly, there is a lot of spandex being worn in the workplace. Tight clothes often lead to unwarranted attention." Jayna's approach to Lululemon's communications challenge in the event of a crisis was simple: full disclosure. "Tell it quickly and tell it honestly," she wrote. Lululemon only partially followed Jayna's advice.

Chapter Ten

RUVIN'S WEIRD FEELING

As Detectives Ruvin and Drewry returned to police headquarters on Monday night, Ruvin was wrestling with his thoughts. The young detective had entered Brittany's apartment believing that she was the victim of a horrible attack; now he was beginning to find Brittany's account leaky and, in some places, downright fantastic.

For one thing, the robbers had no robbery weapons. According to Brittany, they had come into the store empty-handed, except for their masks and gloves. Who robs a store without a weapon? No knives, no guns? All the implements used to kill Jayna belonged to Lululemon. What kind of characters could these guys be?

Another thing didn't compute for Ruvin: the discrepancy between Jayna's massive injuries and Brittany's relatively superficial wounds. Brittany had only required a few stitches. Her injuries were well on their way to healing. The bad guys had brutally killed Jayna, but "they were basically mind-fucking Brittany," said Ruvin. He was having trouble believing that the bad guys were "so cool, calm and collected that they stayed in the store just to mentally torture Brittany."

The whole scenario began to feel made up, said Ruvin. Brittany had already compared the drama to the video game Grand Theft Auto. To fit this script, the bad guys would almost have to be a double incarnation of maximum evil, which he found improbable. "If you're going to make up somebody evil, what are they going to do? They're going to rape, they're going to rob, they're going to kill, they're going to be a racist. It's like you're creating the most evil person in the world. It was like a movie." Ruvin conjectured that it might be possible to "find one Hannibal Lecter," the psychopathic killer portrayed in the 1991 film *The Silence of the Lambs.* "But two guys? That is rare."

In addition to the cinematic feel, the new information Brittany had given the detectives was eroding Ruvin's belief in the two-masked-men scenario. The fact that Brittany had been thrown down atop Jayna's body was a shocker. Brittany's claim that the men knew her name and address was another. And there was the matter of the sneakers: If they belonged to Lululemon, and they matched the bloody footprints in the store, what were the bad guys wearing?

Ruvin and Drewry stopped on their way back to the headquarters for a bathroom break at a firehouse on Georgia Avenue, just inside the Maryland line. Drewry could tell that his sidekick, the young man he'd been mentoring for three years, was getting into some kind of a funk, some kind of a reflective mood. "What's on your mind, Dimitry?" he asked.

At first, Ruvin didn't want to answer, because he had begun thinking the unthinkable. Could it be that Brittany Norwood was not the victim of a crime, but the perpetrator of one? Was it possible that the woman with all the blood on her face two days before, the person who obsessed about the great pools of blood around Jayna was in fact the person who spilled all the blood, including her own? Could the woman who sobbed when describing her own rape by a clothes hanger and asked so gently about "my friend" be a violent attacker? It was such a shocking thought that even Ruvin didn't completely trust his instincts. The idea that one Lululemon staffer had killed another, the murderer small and petite, the victim bigger and more muscular, was more than the intuitive mind could grasp.

"I didn't want to say what I wanted to say—that Brittany killed Jayna," said Ruvin.

But Drewry pressed Ruvin again, so the young detective said it: "This is just crazy. Her story seems so exaggerated. Two really evil guys just doesn't make sense. But does one evil woman make sense?

"I'm beginning to think there weren't any masked men. I'm beginning to think Brittany killed Jayna."

Drewry couldn't believe it. It was so far-fetched, he didn't *want* to believe it.

The other members of the homicide and sex crimes team were waiting at headquarters to hear what Drewry and Ruvin had to report from their interview with Brittany. At first, each man went to his own cubicle in the first-floor warren at headquarters. Ruvin had decided to keep his wild new theory to himself. "I just sat at my computer and I didn't want to say anything. I thought, 'I'll just write up my notes. It is what it is.'"

But after a while, Drewry showed up at Ruvin's desk: "Why don't you come tell everybody what you think?" he said.

The detectives all gathered in an open area called the squad bay. Ruvin retraced his thought process. How could two attackers, not just one, be *so evil*? How do you rob a store without weapons? The whole story seemed like a movie script.

As he talked, Ruvin was becoming increasingly convinced of his theory. "I was getting more and more riled up. I remembered how we found the zip ties used to tie up Brittany. Another officer and I had been standing out by the back door at Lululemon for ten minutes before we happened to notice the zip ties on a shelf. They were in a box with lots of other boxes piled up around them. I'm like, 'They just killed a girl, they're in a panic, how are they so cool that they could think, *Oh, let's look, oh, wow, zip ties, let's zip-tie Brittany*'?"

And something else: "The thing that kind of hit me and gave me some more power was the fact that the footprints never left the store. It bothered us from the beginning that the footprints never left the store. But now, in the context of Brittany being involved, it made sense. The footprints never left the store because the killer never left the store."

Add to all this the fact that the Apple Store managers had heard only two voices, both of them female. Where were the voices of the two bad guys?

"What are you trying to say, Dimitry?"

"I think Brittany killed Jayna. I think she killed her."

The squad bay erupted. "Everybody flipped out and were just, like, 'No way! No fuckin' way this girl did this!'" remembers Ruvin.

But Sergeant Wittenberger, the head of Ruvin's squad, said, "Let's try and look at it this way."

Wittenberger led the way to a computer. For the first time, the detectives began looking at the photos they had of Brittany with a skeptical eye. They had a picture of her lying on her back in the Lululemon bathroom with her bound wrists inexplicably extended over her head. She could have lowered them at any time. She could have crawled to the store's front door. She could have found and used her cell phone.

They had other shots of her in the hospital. They could clearly see her wounds. Wittenberger enlarged the pictures on his screen. The old cop in him came alive. In his long career, he had occasionally seen cases of self-inflicted wounds; Ruvin had not. Wittenberger knew what to look for: lacerations that were only skin deep; cuts in straight lines; parallel cuts. These were exactly the kind of injuries the photos showed on Brittany's body. The emergency room doctor had called almost all of

Brittany's skin lacerations "superficial." She needed stitches only for the gash on her forehead and the cut between her thumb and forefinger. But there was one odd thing: Brittany had cuts on her back, too. How could they be self-inflicted?

Ruvin and Wittenberger tried the obvious: They reached behind their own backs to see if they could touch the spots where Brittany was cut. Yep, it would be easy to make those wounds with your own hand. Wittenberger showed Ruvin what to look for: "If you pull your arm across your back, there's a natural upward motion," he said. Sure enough, Brittany's two back wounds tailed upward.

"For me, it was just like a weird feeling," remembers Ruvin. "These other guys with a lot more experience in crime scenes started looking at things in a new way. By that time, I was convinced...."

Studying the enlarged photos, the cops made another discovery: the cuts in Brittany's pants did not line up with the wounds on her thighs. The thigh cuts must have been made with the pants pulled down, contrary to what Brittany had said. Same thing on top. Brittany had cuts across her breasts, but none in the pink Lululemon top she had been wearing. What about that?

One thing that did line up properly was the crotch of Brittany's pants. It was ripped right in the groin, exposing her genitals.

But there was something odd about that, too. When a rape nurse had gone to the hospital to examine Brittany—standard procedure—she found Brittany's genitals undamaged. She reported "no tears or tenderness" to Brittany's vagina. Lack of evidence does not mean rape has not occurred, she later noted. But given Brittany's story of assault by clothes hanger, the lack of damage was surprising.

Monday had been a long day. The hot suspect, Kevin, had gone cold. The police chief had announced a big manhunt on television. The lead detectives had visited the surviving victim. Dimitry Ruvin, the youngest cop on the case, had had a weird feeling and the world had begun to turn in a new direction.

Midnight came and went. Slowly, the other detectives began to think Ruvin's theory might have validity. In the early hours of Tuesday, the unthinkable was becoming more thinkable.

Chapter Eleven

FORENSICS BLOODHOUNDS

The Lululemon store had been turned into a forensics trove, like an archeological dig, a scene so rich with data that it took days to process it. Bloody shoeprints ran all over the store. Some of the prints had been made by men's shoes—they were much larger than some of the other prints. David McGill, the "track and trail" expert of the police department, thought there would be four sets of prints—but he could only identify two. One set matched Brittany's size 7½ New Balance sneakers. The other set, huge men's prints, matched the size 14 Reeboks without laces that Wittenberger had found on the shoe rack.

McGill noticed two other strange things: Wherever the shoeprints overlapped, the men's shoeprint was always atop the women's shoeprint. This pattern was consistent throughout the store. McGill could only conclude one thing: the bloody men's footprints had been made *after* all the bloody women's footprints, not during a struggle in which they would alternate.

McGill's other surprise lay in the path traveled by the shoeprints. After circulating around the store, they went to a sink in the back room, then stopped in front of a chair. They never left the room. The wearer must have removed the shoes and cleaned them at the sink. Yet a series of bloody shoelace marks on the floor went from the sink and to the center of the store. McGill was able to match these *slap, slap, slap* marks with the laces in Brittany's New Balance shoes. The shoe soles had been cleaned at the sink, but the shoes were then worn out of the back room with the shoelaces still soaked in blood.

A blood splatter expert, William Vosburgh, was brought in to analyze the blood on the walls. Vosburgh concluded that Jayna had been beaten from a standing to a kneeling position, then prostrate in the back hallway near the exit door. By "simple trigonometry," he could deduce the arc of an attacker's swing with a weapon—the wrench, the mannequin peg, the hammer—at various levels on the walls. The scene Vosburgh described corresponded exactly with what the Apple Store employees had heard coming through their wall.

An alert cop in a patrol car had made another key discovery. He found Jayna's car, a two-door Pontiac G5, parked three blocks away in a lot she never used. Blood was on the car's stick shift, the steering wheel and the inside door buttons. The DNA was primarily Brittany's, plus traces of Jayna's. In the back seat, investigators found a black Lululemon cap. "Sweat at least once every day," read an inside seam. The headband was stained with only one person's blood—Brittany's.

Chapter Twelve

JAYNA'S CAR

The cops now had Brittany in their sights, but not in their net. They had only a theory and some circumstantial evidence. They had hints, traces, Ruvin's weird feeling and Drewry's willingness to play it out. They had to get Brittany talking again. They had to test her story.

On Tuesday, Drewry called Brittany's sister, Marissa, to request that Brittany come to police headquarters to give fingerprints and hair samples for DNA "elimination purposes." Elimination is a standard investigative technique to exclude the fingerprints of cops or store employees so investigators can focus on outsiders. In fact, Drewry's elimination story was a ruse.

Drewry really wanted to know what Brittany would say about being in Jayna's car. He was operating under an old detective's maxim: *Please lie to me*. When a suspect delivers what the investigator knows to be a flat-out lie, it shows the investigation is on the right track. "Sometimes, a provable lie is just as good as the truth," said Drewry.

Drewry, the easy-going cop who had worked scores of murders, broken down scores of perps, and heard it all, was in his element. On Wednesday morning, wearing a green sweater-vest, which added a casual touch to his six-foot, two-inch frame, Drewry led Brittany to a small windowless interview room. It was a tight space with gray-carpeted walls and a metal table that clanged loudly into a hidden microphone every time anyone banged on the table top. Brittany didn't know that the room was wired for audio and video. Sitting at the end of the table, Brittany was facing the camera she could not see.

The technicians assigned to collect the fingerprints and hair samples were delayed. Drewry asked how Brittany was doing, if she was considering moving back to Seattle. Since she was about to give a hair sample, he also asked if she had changed her hair since the attack. "I know women don't like to give up your secrets and stuff like that," he noted in his usual downbeat way. Brittany said she had not changed her hair. "I leave my weave the same."

By now, Ruvin had joined them. Drewry changed subjects. Did Brittany know what kind of car Jayna drove?

"I don't. I saw it once. I don't know the make and model."

Later, Drewry asked again: "Has she ever given you a ride home or anything?" (Adding *or anything* and *or stuff like that* were Drewry's favorite softeners for his queries.)

"No," said Brittany.

The detectives knew they had just caught Brittany in her first big lie; her blood had been found in Jayna's car.

Drewry told Brittany that he was hard of hearing in one ear and asked her to speak up—another white lie to get his suspect to talk louder for the secret recording.

Drewry led Brittany back through the full story of the attack five days earlier. She told it all for the third time, complete with sobs and softness. Her story tracked with her two previous versions, including details, descriptions and order. She even rode the same emotional roller-coaster. She included the sexist, racist name-calling: *dirty bitch, dirty nigger.* She included the clothes-hanger rape. She included her fear that her attacker could come after her: "He knows where I live! He tells me that he'll kill me! I'm scared for my life!"

In his avuncular way, Drewry knew how to broach intimate topics. He asked Brittany if she had a boyfriend and if she had had sex lately. Drewry suggested they might need a DNA sample from her sex partner to "eliminate him from any semen that would have been left behind by the bad guy."

"There wouldn't have been any semen inside me anyway," Brittany said with almost scientific certainty. After all, the rapist had entered her only briefly, and a clothes hanger leaves no semen. Besides, she said, she had not had sex in more than a week before the assault.

Drewry and Ruvin knew differently. They knew that the nurse's examination of Brittany, while not providing any evidence of rape, had revealed something else: Brittany *did* have semen traces that were less than a week old. A couple of Lululemon girls had told investigators that Brittany had been out with a former college basketball player she met in the store—and that she told them she had sex with him just two days before the Lululemon attack.

The detectives knew they had now caught Brittany in two lies. She must have been in Jayna's car: Brittany's blood had been found inside. And she had had sex during the previous week, but now she was denying it. She was trying, in a convoluted way, to negate the negative results of the rape test. Instead, she had walked into another trap, lying about her sex life.

The net around Brittany was tightening, but not yet enough. The detectives could not pounce. So far they had only a theory and a couple of lies. As they sent Brittany home, they were wondering how they could get her back.

Chapter Thirteen

'THAT'S NOT POSSIBLE!'

While the rest of the world was feverishly searching for two masked men in black, Drewry and Ruvin were thinking about how to build a stronger forensic case around Brittany. At the same time, they hoped she might be induced to tell the truth, to confess to the murder and explain how it happened. After all, she was talkative and had woven a complex story. Many of its elements seemed realistic, plausible and nuanced, right down to nitty-gritty details. Maybe she could be drawn into more lies. But how to get her to talk again?

Brittany did it for them. She offered to return to police headquarters. On Thursday, her brother, Chris, and her sister, Marissa, called Drewry. Brittany wanted to get something else off her chest, they said. She had not told the detectives everything in the last meeting. The detectives couldn't believe their luck. Ruvin knew they were in for a confrontational meeting with Brittany.

On Friday morning, Brittany sat down in the sound-proofed interview room right across from the hidden camera. Chris and Marissa waited outside. Brittany then uncorked the newest twist in her convoluted tale. Saying that she was racked with insomnia and emotional overload, Brittany came straight to the point: She hadn't been forthcoming in their last conversation about Jayna's car. Not only had she been inside the car, she had actually driven it! On the night of the attack! The attackers had made her do it!

The detectives knew they had now been catapulted onto a new level of the absurd. This was a reach into Neverland, an unexpected degree of stagecraft. If it were not so tragic, Brittany's convoluted choreography would have made great entertainment.

Drewry and Ruvin kept their poker faces. The masked men had *made* Brittany drive Jayna's car? Where? When?

"Prior to him sexually assaulting me and zip-tying me, they made me move her car," she said. She had driven it to a parking lot on "the other side of Wisconsin [Avenue]," she said—the exact spot where Jayna's car had been found. "They said that if I was to pass anyone and open my mouth, I can consider myself dead. And that one of them would be watching me the entire time. I remember seeing a cop and I was just too scared to even flag him down."

Brittany sobbed and danced around a series of questions from Drewry. The masked men gave no reason for telling her to move Jayna's car, she said. Drewry mused aloud: "People would probably ask, 'Well, why didn't you just keep on going and not go back?'"

Brittany: "Because they knew where I lived! I was scared for my life!"

The story thickened. Brittany claimed that she had passed people on the street while returning to the store. Drewry asked: "Did they kind of look at you funny or anything like that, you know, 'Whoa, what's she doing all bloody?'"

"I was walking this way and they were coming this way," said Brittany, indicating a criss-cross.

"What did they say?"

"Nothing."

Drewry tried again: "Did they kind of look at you funny like, you know, it *is* Bethesda, a black girl with blood all over her...?"

"I don't know if they saw."

Drewry, in his downbeat style, drifted casually away from the car story and began walking Brittany through the attack again. She was consistent through most of it—remembering which side of her head she had been struck on, for instance, in previous tellings of her story. She offered the detail that while moving the car, she wore a black hat; investigators had found a blood-stained black hat in Jayna's car.

In her touchingly sobbing way, Brittany added details: One of the masked men was wearing a sweatshirt with a hood and a zipped coat that made noise "like a swishy material." His pants were nylon running pants. He wore black tennis shoes.

Brittany was now fully in character. A rape victim who'd been through hell, she filled her role like a method actress; she lived the emotions of the victim she had created. When she described being "punched" by her attacker, her voice squeaked with the remembered pain. Her story had urgency. When Drewry began putting a little pressure on her, she replied with tearful defiance: "Do you know how many times they hit me in the head?" she screeched. When Drewry sounded incredulous that the bad guys would tell her to move Jayna's car, she pressed back: "I'm not safe! I know you say that [these] people never come back, but I don't want to take the chance!"

Drewry asked about the details of the rape. "How long was he inside you with his penis? Was he hard, was he erect? Or couldn't he get it up?"

"He was hard," she replied softly, like a woman reliving her own assault.

Drewry asked again where the attack on Jayna had begun. In one of the bathrooms opposite the changing stalls, said Brittany. Was Jayna face down while he was hitting her? asked the detective.

"Maybe on her knees," replied Brittany, echoing the blood splatter expert's description of Jayna's slow descent into death. After she was forced into the back hallway, said Brittany, she could hear Jayna only "faintly"—an exact reprise of the Apple employees' recollection of Jayna's fading voice in her dying moments.

Ruvin and Drewry took a break then returned. It was time for the end game. Drewry asked if Jayna had moved at all when the attackers pushed Brittany on top of her. "She moved when I fell on her but she didn't say anything," answered Brittany.

"She was probably dying, right?" said Drewry. Brittany nodded fast and began sobbing loudly.

A silence. Drewry folded his arms and sat back.

Then he pounced. "Brittany, comes a point sometimes when we have to break down and get everything off of our chests. I'm sure that you have been going absolutely nuts for these past couple of days, with worry, with fear [about] what the cops have figured out. You gotta be! You got to tell us what really happened. Because I know what really happened."

Brittany: "I told you what really happened!"

Drewry: "No. You've concocted an incredible story that doesn't make any doggone sense."

"No!"

"I've been a cop for over 30 years. ...I've seen a lot of stuff. I've heard a lot of tales."

Brittany denied everything. She denied that her wounds were self-inflicted. She denied that she was just posing when she held her arms over her head while lying on the Lululemon bathroom floor. She denied that she and Jayna might have had a confrontation.

"So why did you kill her, then?"

"I didn't!"

"Yes, you did."

"No, I didn't! I would never do that. Jayna was my friend!"

"Okay, then who did kill her? 'Cause there were not two guys in there."

"Yes, there were!"

Caught, trapped, busted, Brittany was in full-blown denial. She seemed to believe the fiction she had been selling for a week. Her mind was in the parallel universe she'd created. Her responses for the next half-hour fit her self-delusion.

Drewry and Ruvin used every device they could imagine to get Brittany to admit the murder. They told her they knew how hard it was to deal with all this. They could feel the emotional state she must be in. Drewry said he believed she needed psychological help.

The 61-year-old policeman tried cajoling the 28-year-old woman in his most paternal style: "Come on, baby, you gotta tell me."

Nothing worked. Drewry even tried shifting some of the blame to Jayna, conjuring an even fight between the two women. "I don't think that you meant to kill her. I think that shit went south real fast, for whatever reason, and you went off, and that she went off on you, too."

"I told you what happened!" she shot back.

"No. You told me what you want us to think happened."

Ruvin jumped in. He gave Brittany the easiest out: "Brittany, we know you're a good person. You did something in the heat of the moment. You panicked. You started making stuff up. Anybody in your position would have tried to ... cover it up. That shows that you are a human being and you have a guilty conscience."

No luck.

Ruvin even invented a story about himself, saying that as a youngster he once broke his parents' VCR and tried to cover up his action by simply removing the unit from the house as though it had never existed.

Still no luck.

Ruvin followed Drewry's tactic. "What I don't know is, why the fight happened between you and Jayna," said Ruvin. "Was she pissed? Did she call you a name? The whole thing about the N-word...."

Drewry: "Did she smack you first?" Drewry slammed his hands together loudly, imitating a slap. "'Bitch! What the fuck!'"

Finally, Drewry drew his chair up close to Brittany's. In his low, confiding voice, he told her: "You've got to get this off your chest, baby. You got to. It's tearing you up inside. Your stomach has got to be all in knots."

"I just want to go home," she sobbed.

"Why don't you tell us what happened and then you can go home," lied Drewry. He knew Brittany was not going home on this day.

"I told you everything," she croaked.

"You told us a fabulous lie."

The cops couldn't budge Brittany. Drewry decided it was time to ratchet up the pressure. "Okay," he said. "I'm going to have to get Chris and Marissa in here.

Either I'm going to tell them [what happened] or you're going to tell them."

Brittany said nothing.

* * *

Drewry read Brittany her Miranda rights, reminding her that she had the right to be silent, the right to a lawyer and that anything she said could be used against her. Drewry did it in his casual way, saying it was just "a formality." Then he brought Chris and Marissa into the cramped room.

In the next half-hour, Brittany's story and her life fell apart. Her brother and sister were crushed by the full force of the evidence against Brittany. "I'm freakin' the fuck out," groaned Chris mid-story.

For Marissa, it was too much. She went into near-shock when Drewry, after ticking off the fakes and flaws in Brittany's story, after showing photos of Brittany's self-inflicted wounds, finally said: "Brittany killed Jayna."

"That's not possible!" gasped Marissa.

Brittany vigorously shook her head.

"But it's true," said Drewry.

Marissa wiped her hands over her face. "This is not...this is not...."

Drewry: "But it is."

Ruvin pointed out that the staffers in the Apple Store had heard only two voices during the altercation in Lululemon, both women's, none men's.

Turning to Chris, Drewry said, "I was hoping that, with your help, Brittany might be willing to tell us what happened and why."

Brittany remained mute, refusing the bait. Marissa began breaking down in sobs. Chris asked that she be taken out of the room. Ruvin led Marissa out, but her wail could be heard through the closed door.

Drewry reminded Chris that, during their Monday night visit to Brittany's apartment, Chris wondered why his sister had been only slightly injured while Jayna was brutally murdered. His gut had told him something was wrong with that picture.

"There were things that didn't add up," Chris admitted now. He had suspected Brittany might be in cahoots with her own alleged attackers. "I was concerned that the assailants ... [that] there was a connection. You guys have convinced yourselves that Brittany did it."

"The evidence," rebutted Drewry. "I did not want to believe it at first. *I did not want to believe it.*"

Brittany looked down. Chris said: "Naturally, I don't want to believe it. I'm Brittany's brother and I love her. You can't expect me to turn my back on my little sister. I could get defensive. I could come up with something like, 'Oh, we're in Montgomery County, this is Bethesda, they need a story. They need to solve this....'"

Drewry: "Yeah, and throw the black girl under the bus...."

Chris: "No, I'm not saying it's a race thing, I'm thinking a socio-economic thing. Nobody wants people that are afraid. There's little ladies in boutiques in Bethesda saying, 'Oh, my God, I'm not working at night'—things like that. And as soon as the police can restore order in the area, everyone's happy. [But] I'm not saying that."

Drewry told Chris about Jayna's car. Chris was increasingly incredulous. He could only explain her fanciful cover-up as an act of fearful and muddled thinking. "She's a little girl and she's scared shitless. Maybe she was stupid about it," he said

Brittany sat silently.

Chris walked through the same thought process that would occupy minds for weeks and months later. Why would Brittany create an impossible cover-up? Speaking to Drewry, he laid out what a more logical criminal mind would think:

"Say I killed Jayna. I'm going to collect the DNA. I'm going to change clothes in the Lululemon store. I'm going to take everything of mine that has DNA on it and burn it. I'm going to leave. I could have left in [Jayna's] car."

Brittany still said nothing.

Drewry picked up on the story. "I'm sure she was thinking just that same thought," he said. A policeman had seen someone in Jayna's car in the parking lot in the middle of the night. The passenger stayed in the car for more than an hour. DNA showed that the passenger was Brittany. She must be thinking, said Drewry, "What do I do? What kind of a story do I come up with? Do I change clothes and run off and have it so that Jayna was attacked inside the store by herself? Or do I go back and say that we were both attacked? Those are the only two options."

Ruvin: "When a little girl is in that position, she's going to get scared, and she's going to create all that... because she doesn't want, even to herself, to believe that this happened."

Drewry turned again to Brittany: "So what happened, Brittany?

"I told you."

"You didn't tell us the truth. You need to tell us the truth. I know you're in turmoil."

Seated in the corner, looking down most of the time, Brittany said nothing.

Chris asked the detectives, "Can I talk to her for a minute, alone?"

Drewry and Ruvin left the room.

Chapter Fourteen

'DID YOU?'

C hris leaned back against a door. He was sitting only two feet from Brittany.

In a low voice, he said: "Should I ask you? Did you?"

Brittany: "I don't want to talk about it here. I just want to go home."

Chris: "I don't know if they are going to let you go. Just tell me right now. Did you do it? Because if you did, we have to get you a lawyer to defend you. And it's going to be a fucking media shitstorm. So you need to tell me right now if you did."

Brittany feared the room might be bugged. She said, "I just don't want to talk about it here."

Chris: "Listen. They're not going to let us go. Just nod your head if you did it. Please tell me. ...Please."

Brittany looked down but didn't nod. "I just don't want everybody to be disappointed in me," she said.

"No one's disappointed in you—we're your family! No matter what, we're going to be here for you...."

Chris leaned forward, looking at Brittany: "Everything he just told me, and I didn't look like I was convinced—*but that is really fucking convincing*. You are going to have to just tell me so I can at least try to get you out of here. This is going to get a helluva lot fucking worse."

Brittany: "Sorry."

Chris: "Don't apologize."

Brittany: "[*garbled*]."

Chris: "You're not going to [*garbled*]? Okay, I'll take that as a yes."

No response from Brittany.

Chris: "Why?"

Brittany: "I don't know how it happened."

Chris: "Was it shoplifting? Were you trying to steal?"

Brittany: "No."

"Then why did you fight this girl? You tell me. I can think on my feet and I can help deflect these guys. But I need information before I can do that."

Brittany leaned an elbow on the table and looked toward the wall: "Are you sure they can't hear us, Chris?"

Glancing up at the ceiling, Chris said: "I've looked around for listening devices. There's nothing in this room. Even if they did, it's nothing they can use in court."

Leaning towards Brittany, Chris whispered: "So, just tell me....what happened? You don't have to give me details, just tell me why this happened. Was the whole thing planned or did...."

Brittany, wailing: "Nooo! Not at all, Chris."

Chris: "So what did she do? Tell me what she did to get you to fight her."

Brittany was crying. "I really did forget my wallet."

"I believe that. Did she accuse you of shoplifting? Is that what it's all about? Yes?"

"I didn't take anything."

"Okay, listen. Here's what we're going to do. ...We're going to have to get you a defense attorney. We have two options. [There is] temporary insanity, but you've talked to too many people. You've talked to counselors and people know that you're not insane. ...That's not going to work. You're going to have to be very honest with us and the attorney. We're going to have to try to concoct some sort of plan—like she attacked you. But that doesn't look good because you tried to cover it all up."

Almost whispering, Chris sighed: "Oh, God..."

Brittany remained silent, looking at the floor.

Suddenly she broke into a fast, sobbing, nearly unintelligible soliloquy. "Chris, I'm sorry! I don't know what to say, Chris. ... I didn't know what to do. ...I honestly ... happened. ...Chris, *I didn't know what to do!*"

Chris: "I know you didn't."

Brittany: "Chris I have never been accused of anything. ...I've been doing so well...I...have a job..."

A few seconds later, Chris asked: "She came to let you in, right? Then what? What did she say?"

Brittany: "That she was gonna make sure our manager knew, or something."

Chris: "...the manager knew what, that you were shoplifting?"

Brittany: "But I wasn't..."

Chris: "Had you stolen from that store before?"

Brittany: "*Never.* Chris, honestly, I was doing good. ...I mean, as far as..."

Chris: "I believe you. ...Okay [deep sigh, hangs his head]...I'm trying to keep my head, I'm trying to be cool. I want you to be cool with me."

Brittany: "I'm worse than ever...."

Chris: "Stop! You're our family and we're trying to protect you. That's what's important—protecting you. I'm going to go talk to the cops and see what we can do."

But before he left the room, Chris offered his sister a startling piece of advice: She needed to learn how to lie to the police.

Chris: "Now, listen. You've done it three times. When the cops ask you a question, you're looking down and you're looking to your left. That means that you're lying. If you're going to lie when you talk to them, find something in the room. See that red button? [*He points at a red button on a wall.*] Look at that red button every time. Do not look at anything else. I watched you. Every time, your head drops down to your left. That immediately tells everyone that you're lying. [*whispering*] I lie all the time so I know these things, okay?"

Brittany: "Are they allowed to record this?"

Chris: "There's no recording devices in here. I was looking around the room the entire time. See that thing on the wall?" Chris points at an innocuous metal faceplate.

As he stood to leave the room, Chris stared directly at a different metal plate on a different wall. He did not realize he was looking directly into the hidden camera.

* * *

Just down the hall, behind closed doors, Drewry and Ruvin were watching intently on a closed-circuit monitor as Brittany unloaded her tangled tale to her brother. They were surrounded by the police brass, people way above their pay grade. The cops were witnessing something unprecedented: the semi-confession of a young woman involved in a massive explosion of violence and a bizarre range of playacting that they'd never seen before.

The conversation between Brittany and Chris lasted seven minutes, but it was clear almost immediately that Brittany could not be allowed to leave police headquarters as a free woman. The moment of truth had arrived. It was time to close the net around Brittany.

At 1:54 p.m., one week to the day after Jayna Murray died, Drewry arrested Brittany for killing Jayna.

Within hours, the pictures were running on the evening news: Brittany in handcuffs being led to a police car. She was headed for her first night behind bars. The news tore through Washington like a cannon shot—nobody saw it coming. The police chief had announced a full-bore manhunt only four days earlier. Now he was proclaiming the crime solved with the arrest of a young colleague of Jayna's. Like everyone else, the chief had been a victim of Brittany's amazing storytelling. He had joined the entire community in what State's Attorney McCarthy would later call a "willing suspension of disbelief."

In Bethesda, people were dumbfounded that the grisly act could have been committed by a college-educated Lululemon woman. *A woman couldn't do that!* thought Margarita Lisi, a server at Parker's, an Irish bar on Bethesda Avenue where Lululemon girls sometimes went for after-work drinks.

In their shock, Bethesdans issued a collective sigh of relief. They felt a muted joy that a single perpetrator, however despicable, had been found. The murder was an aberration, not a new trend in urban pathology. No two men in black had invaded the tranquil precincts of suburban life. The bubble had not been pierced. The murder in the yoga store was an unexplainable descent into hell, not likely to be repeated. The world was safe again—more or less.

Chapter Fifteen

FUNERAL

As Brittany was being handcuffed and moved to jail, nearly 200 people were gathering 1,400 miles away, just outside Houston, to say goodbye to Jayna. It had been a single horrible week, almost to the hour, since her shooting-star life had ended. Fraser, her fiancé-to-be, flew in from Seattle. Matt came from Portland, Oregon. Leah crossed half the country from San Diego. Jayna's brother, Hugh, a lawyer in the U.S. Army, had flown home from Iraq. Even Chip Wilson, Lululemon's Canadian founder, and Christine Day, its CEO, flew to Houston.

As the Murray family drove to the cemetery chapel in a memorial park under live oaks and tall pines, the Murrays received a phone call. It was Detective Drewry, calling from Maryland. "We are about to do a press conference," he said. "There has been an arrest."

Phyllis Murray was instantly elated. "Our first reaction was: 'Thank goodness!'" she said. Then Drewry told her who had been arrested: Brittany. Phyllis and the family were "thrown back into shock. Lululemon people didn't do things like this. They were all outstanding people. When we arrived at the wake, I was in tears. We went absolutely numb. That's the only way you can get through something like this. It was surreal."

Wilson and Day, the twin peaks of the Lululemon empire, were no doubt in shock, too. Now the devil was in the door. The evil had come from within. One of their own employees was not just the woman who lay dead before them, but the murderer as well. What could it mean for the company's liability?

As the sad evening progressed, the Murrays were in a free fall of disbelief and rage. They'd never even heard of Brittany Norwood before last week. It was too much to process. "I just went blank," said Hugh. "I don't even remember who I talked to that day."

But other people at the gathering were talking. They talked about how Jayna's 30 years had been exceptionally full. They told how she had enriched their lives, lit up their moods, led them to believe in themselves. The girl with the mega-smile, the daredevil and world traveler, the natural athlete and yoga practitioner, who probably could take down a person twice her size in a fair fight, had—in the eyes of her "faith-based family," as David called his brood—gone to heaven. "She's with our grandchild in heaven, waiting for the transfer of the soul," said Phyllis, referring to the baby expected to be born soon to Hugh's wife, Kate.

Jayna's passage on Earth ended that weekend in a lonely plot in a new section of the cemetery. In time, it will be full of gravestones like Jayna's. Under a Celtic cross, it read: *Until we meet again, may God hold you in the palm of His hand.*

Chapter Sixteen

GOING FOR THE MAX

Seven months had passed since Brittany was led away in handcuffs. She had spent those long days and nights in the Montgomery County lock-up, talking to a counselor, getting involved in the self-help programs, worrying about her hair and nails. "We listened to her jail phone calls," said prosecutor McCarthy. "She was obsessed with grooming. Everything is about getting her nails done, getting her hair done."

While Brittany waited, Bethesda waited, the county waited, everyone waited to find out the details of Brittany's brutal acts, and why she had done them. Would she be convicted of Jayna's murder based on the mass of forensic evidence? Would her secretly recorded words to Detectives Drewry and Ruvin and to her brother guarantee a conviction? Or would she somehow beat the rap? As the prosecutors knew, stranger things have happened.

McCarthy and Ayres worked tirelessly putting together the case against Brittany. The prosecutors felt they had a hard road ahead. They had decided to go for the max—first-degree murder. Getting a conviction would require not only proof that Brittany had killed Jayna, but convincing proof of premeditation—evidence that Brittany had acted with cunning and guile, that she knew what she was doing, that she had not committed a crime of passion.

Beyond getting a first-degree conviction, the prosecution also wanted to get the toughest possible sentence: life in prison *without* the possibility of parole (the death penalty was not an option under Maryland law). Since the judge would decide the sentence, the prosecutors would have to convince not only the jury but also the judge that Brittany's crime was so heinous as to be beyond redemption and rehabilitation.

McCarthy and Ayres had a great case—circumstantially. There was a mountain of evidence—the bloody shoeprints in the store, Brittany's blood in Jayna's car, the blood-spattered walls, the self-inflicted wounds on Brittany's body, the sound of two women's voices (and no men's voices) penetrating the wall into the Apple Store. But there was no smoking gun. The evidence created a narrative, not ironclad proof. There was only one living eyewitness and she wasn't talking.

It would have been far easier to work out a plea bargain. Brittany's attorney, Douglas Wood, a rangy, gray-haired criminal lawyer, had hinted at making a deal that would include committing Brittany to the state mental hospital prison on grounds of temporary insanity. Or she could plead guilty to second-degree murder, which carries a maximum sentence of 30 years with the possibility of parole much sooner than that.

Both the prosecution and the Murray family wanted to bring the full weight of the law down on Brittany—even though a jury trial would put the Murrays through the hell of reliving Jayna's death. There was also the possibility of a bad outcome, such as a hung jury or even an acquittal for lack of hard proof.

"We knew going to trial was a risk," said Hugh. "In a trial, things happen. Remember O. J. Simpson?"

The Murrays also believed it was important that Brittany be put away forever, that she was a sociopath. "Someday she would be cornered again," said Phyllis. "We didn't want anyone to ever face that risk."

But there was another reason that the wounded Murray family wanted a jury trial: They had an abiding yearning to know what really happened, to wrestle their way emotionally through the murder, to travel with Jayna on her last journey.

"The trial was my last opportunity to hear my sister speak," remembers Jayna's brother, Dirk. "The trial spoke volumes. Jayna was trying to help a fellow human being. She was trying to give Brittany her farecard."

"As much as I didn't want to, I needed to know details," said her father, David, a former U.S. Army Special Forces officer during the Vietnam War.

McCarthy and Ayres decided to roll the dice with a jury trial.

* * *

Brittany's trial began, just as the murder investigation had, as a media circus. A crowd mobbed the courthouse in Rockville, Maryland. Passing through a police line holding back onlookers, said Hugh, was "like going into a rock concert." Cameras were everywhere. Reporters were tweeting in the hallways and getting replies from as far away as the Middle East. "People were following this trial around the world," said Washington television reporter Andrea McCarren in amazement. "The Twitter universe was bigger than the TV audience."

A palpable tension permeated the courtroom as the two stricken families—the Murrays and the Norwoods—sat down on opposite sides of the aisle. Throughout the trial, the two families never formally met. The only communication between them was a chance encounter. Said Phyllis: "When I first saw them, my heart just sank. We were numb. And I knew they were having a horrible time. When I ran into the mother and a sister outside the ladies' room, they apologized for our loss. They asked about our grandchildren."

The Murrays still shook their heads at the recollection that they had almost sent flowers of sympathy to Brittany while she was still in the hospital, even as Jayna's body still lay in the rear hallway at Lululemon. They had not sent the flowers only because they had been told that Brittany did not want any.

During the seven months leading up to the trial, the Murrays had spent hours and days listening to McCarthy and Ayres plan their case. McCarthy had intentionally shielded them from many of the worst particulars, especially the autopsy report. He had advised them never to look at the 37 autopsy photographs provided by Dr. Ripple.

The family's grief was matched only by their anger. Hugh remembers walking into the courtroom and laying eyes on Brittany Norwood. "The first time I saw Brittany, I remember thinking, 'She's a small girl, she's a sorry piece of shit.'"

One of Jayna's closest Houston friends, Melissa, flew with the Murrays from Texas for the trial. Like so many others, she had been devastated by Jayna's murder. She spent nearly a week in bed afterwards. Even 18 months later, Melissa—a woman who does not normally talk to herself—found herself shouting "Fucking bitch!" whenever she thought of Brittany while driving down the highway. Like the Murrays, Melissa had to know what really happened. In the courtroom, she wanted to climb into Brittany's brain, to somehow understand the evil coils that led to her violence. "I was just staring at her, saying to myself, 'I want her to look at me.'"

But Brittany, petite and pretty, impeccably dressed and groomed, sometimes wearing pearls as if for a job interview, remained stony-faced, looking straight ahead or down at the table. Anyone who sought a trace of emotion from her for the next six days was disappointed. Indeed, her appearance as a girl-next-door brought the clang of cognitive dissonance. Says Hugh: "There was disbelief. She did not look like a murderer. She is athletic, she doesn't drool, she isn't a mouth-breather. We felt disbelief that she could do that to Jayna."

Like everyone else, Hugh—a former professional triathlete—was astonished that Brittany, at five feet, three inches and 123 pounds, could have overpowered Jayna, at five feet, five inches and 160 pounds. Jayna's weight seemed high for a woman, but that's because Jayna was all muscle. She did not look heavy. She was strong, exceptionally fit, unafraid. She'd been a gymnast, a dancer and a discus thrower as a teen. Now she was a runner, she practiced yoga and she frequently worked out on resistance equipment at CrossFit, her favorite gym in Bethesda. Hugh could still remember Jayna doing wall push-ups at home—her feet against the wall, hands on the floor, pushing up and then touching one hip with one hand.

Jayna's girlfriends remembered her as "muscley" and beautiful. Both traits were captured in a photo taken one warm day on the Washington Mall by Jayna's friend, Marisa. It shows Jayna in yoga pants and a tank top behind a field of white tulips. She's in a classic yoga "tree" pose, hands pressed together, one bare foot on the opposite knee. She flashes her famous smile. Her form is perfect; her strength is obvious in her arms and shoulders. She seems in a state of bliss, at the nexus of a life that is coming together in all the right ways. The photo would later hang as a memorial in Lululemon, not far from the spot where Jayna suffered her fatal blows.

The first blow, thought Hugh, must have been a sucker punch from behind, probably with the steel clothing rod, which left an indentation on the back of Jayna's head. From then on, Jayna's ability to defend herself was compromised.

Chapter Seventeen

DEATH TRAP

The trial was as riveting as the investigation—and lasted just as long. Six grim days were filled with chilling testimony, a drumbeat of evidence and the drama of the detectives' sleuthing. Detective Ruvin told of his misplaced suspicions of a man named Kevin—who turned out to have nothing to do with the murder. The young detective related his gnawing doubts about Brittany's story, his feeling of watching a movie. Detective Drewry took the stand for half a day and commented on the secretly recorded interviews he and Ruvin had with Brittany. Forensics experts unveiled complex calculations of "blood cast-off" and shoeprint patterns. Dr. Ripple, the medical examiner, detailed Jayna's 331 wounds. Lululemon girls with quavering voices and shaking hands recounted their stories. The two Apple Store employees told of hearing Jayna's pleas for help through their wall, and of her voice finally fading into nothing—even as they did nothing.

With 25 witnesses and more than 200 exhibits, the trial was like experiencing the murder in slow motion. Every moment of Jayna's suffering and Brittany's deception was stretched into hours. Each twist and turn was vivid and painful. The families took the emotional blows, day after day, one gut-wrenching detail after the other.

"Every day we left there saying, 'I had no idea, I didn't know that,'" remembers Hugh. "It was exhausting. We were strung out, not sleeping, eating poorly."

For the Norwoods, the trial was torment of another kind. They had to listen as their daughter was described as a monster, a torturer, a mutilator. They had to see photographs of what Brittany did to Jayna's skull and face. They had to hear John McCarthy, the state's attorney, say on the first day of the trial that Brittany "savagely ended the life of Jayna Murray."

With those words hanging in the air, defense attorney Wood took the courtroom floor and began his opening statement. He talked about Brittany's big family, her soccer background and her work at Lululemon. He claimed Jayna and Brittany had worked together without conflicts or altercations. Then, he said, when the two women returned to the store on that fateful Friday night, "there was a horrific fight." Things got out of hand.

Finally, he said, "Jayna was killed by Brittany."

The courtroom gasped. Brittany did it? Was the trial over? Phyllis Murray remembers seeing some of the jurors gathering their things, as if to go home.

But it was not as simple as that. Yes, said Brittany's attorney, she had "caused the death of Jayna Murray." But, he argued, Brittany was not guilty of first degree murder. Hers was not an act of premeditation. Instead, "she lost it. She lost control."

Even if true, the idea of a horrific fight between Brittany and Jayna was supposition. Yet the defense needed a narrative that skirted premeditation. If a conflict had started as a fair fight over something—nobody was saying what—and then veered into a crime of passion, Brittany might get only a second-degree murder conviction.

Brittany's attorney was clearly playing the crazy card without calling it insanity. Before the trial, he had hinted at an insanity defense, but never followed up—probably because there was not enough evidence of clinically insane behavior in Brittany's life to support it. Still, defense attorney Wood's new "lost it" argument had a certain internal logic: Brittany certainly seemed to have lost control. Even some of the Lululemon girls believed that is what happened. "She didn't mean to kill Jayna," said one. "She lost it and there was no turning back."

* * *

Whether Brittany lost it or acted in the full knowledge of what she was doing may never truly be known. But what she did, and the probable order in which she did it, was dramatically laid out over the next six days.

The defense attorney's admission that Brittany killed Jayna was only a partial game-changer. The prosecution no longer had to prove that Brittany committed homicide. But they still had to show premeditation and such brutality that Brittany should never have the possibility of parole. Their story had to be awful. It was.

According to the prosecution narrative, Brittany's attack began in Lululemon's back room, since the steel merchandise pegs were kept there in a bucket. "Here's your murder weapon," a forensic expert had told McCarthy and Ayres, comparing the end of the peg with a wound to Jayna's head. Jayna dropped her bag on the first blow, then rushed towards the front of the store but made it only as far as the flat screen TV opposite the fitting rooms. Jayna knocked over the TV and left her bloody palm print on the wall. Clumps of her blond hair, severed by blows from the steel rod, fell on the floor. Jayna then ran out of her black jacket—Brittany was probably grabbing it; the jacket was found in the same area as the TV.

Jayna lunged for the rear exit. She made it into the narrow rear hallway, and may have left her bloody handprint on the rear pushbar. Her cell phone, busted open, was found on the floor nearby.

Finally, Jayna was cornered at the opposite end of the little hallway—literally a dead end. It was in that "death trap," as Ayres called it, that the ultimate confrontation occurred. It was there that the screaming women were overheard by the Apple Store employees. It was there that Brittany continued pummeling Jayna until she collapsed to her knees, then fell flat on the floor, and died under Brittany's unrelenting blows and stabs.

* * *

Jayna was dead. Brittany was alive. Now the murderer went into phase two of her ghoulish act. She conjured an operatic story of cartoonish proportions, a Grand Guignol that finally exceeded its own dramatic limitations.

The fabrication began with Brittany's decision to move Jayna's car. Parking was tight on Bethesda Avenue; Jayna's silver Pontiac was probably in a no-parking zone since she thought she would be in Lululemon for only a few minutes. Brittany knew the illegally parked car would draw attention. At 12:30 a.m., two hours after the murder, a policeman noticed someone sitting in a silver car in a parking lot three blocks from Lululemon, its headlights on. More than two hours later, the car was still there, the headlights still on—though the policeman did not notice if anyone was in the car.

However long Brittany sat in the parking lot, argued McCarthy, it gave her time to conjure the fiction that would become her new reality: an intrusion from outside the store, an attack by two men in black. The assault would be violent and nasty, the work of crazed criminals who defiled and mistreated women with word and action. Since she was black, the attack would be racist, including repeated use of the word *nigger*. Most important, it would include rape, since that would divert suspicion completely from Brittany. And she would have the man rape her with a clothes hanger, since that would leave no sperm and no DNA evidence. She would be home free.

Returning to the store, Brittany created a new crime scene atop the old one. She soaked her shoes in the swamp of Jayna's blood, then tracked them around the store. She then donned the men's size 14 Reeboks and did the same thing again. Now a crazy pattern of mayhem was laid across the floor—a "chicken dance" of shoeprints, as the prosecution called it.

Afterwards, Brittany washed both pairs of shoes in the back room sink. She placed the men's shoes back on the store's rack. She didn't notice that the shoelaces of her own shoes were still bloody and left little slap marks on the floor as she walked away from the sink, another critical clue for the forensic specialists. Topping off the scene-doctoring, Brittany flung clothing and other objects—hangers, a broom, a mop, a chair—around, creating false mayhem, easily identified by the forensic scientists as "late arrivals"—calculated, after-the-fact placements into the crime scene.

Now Brittany went beyond plot invention and creative stagecraft. She had to have the sheer physical guts and commitment to her new reality to slash herself with a razor blade—her breasts, stomach, thighs, back and face. She also cut her pants, but not in exactly the right places. She forgot to cut her top, which later exposed her lies when she described her attack.

Finally, using zip ties from a shelf near Jayna's body, Brittany neatly bound her ankles and, using her teeth, zip-tied her wrists. (A forensic expert demonstrated how easily it could be done.) Her staging was complete. She lay down amid broken glass and blood spatter in the bathroom and pretended to black out.

As diabolical as it was, Brittany's dark drama worked magnificently at first. It was plausible, well-constructed, backed up with evidence—the clothes hanger, the footprints, the dropped bags, the open cash registers. It was told with feeling. "This woman was a phenomenal actress," said McCarthy. "She whimpers and cries on cue." Added Judge Greenberg: "You're a helluva liar, ma'am. An entire community was terrorized."

Because of its extremism, it was hard for most people to imagine that Brittany's tale might be a trumped-up story. "You just don't think that a woman is going to expose her vagina, cut her breasts and her legs," said Ayres. "It's just so pathological, the level of deception, that [a cover-up] is just not what people are going to immediately think. As human beings, we want to believe it's the masked men. You don't want to believe it's the articulate, educated, attractive girl next door."

Once Brittany's story fell apart and its gaudy seams showed, many people thought that the cops and investigators must have seen through her fabrication all along. Hindsight got a good ride with folks who were not working the case, who didn't walk into the crime scene and find all the pieces exactly as Brittany described them from her hospital bed. They had not seen the Apple Store video of two men in black walking from the direction of Lululemon. "We had a picture of the bad guys!" remembers McCarthy. Those men later turned out to be dishwashers leaving their shift at a nearby restaurant.

But for two critical mistakes—leaving the men's sneakers in the store and moving Jayna's car—Brittany's fabulous lie could have carried the day. "If the police hadn't found the sneakers, Brittany might have gotten away with it," said Ayres. "She could have just dumped the shoes somewhere."

Expressions of concern for Jayna were among Brittany's cleverest and most despicable diversions. "Can you tell me how my friend is doing?" she had asked Detective Mackie in the hospital. "She was so innocent!" Brittany had wailed during one interview, a queen of crocodile tears.

* * *

After six exhausting days of testimony—during which the defense never called a witness—the lawyers went into closing arguments. McCarthy could no longer shield the Murrays from the full story. For the first time, they experienced Jayna's slow death, blow by blow. For nearly an hour, McCarthy and Ayres reprised the evidence, the testimony, the probable sequence of events. The Murrays' worst fears—worse than their nightmares—were realized. Jayna had not died early in the attack. She had suffered a long and unimaginable torture.

Sitting near the rear of the courtroom, the Murrays hit bottom. Jayna's father, David, the strapping former Texas Aggies linebacker, the stony ex-Special Forces officer who'd looked death in the eye more than once in Southeast Asia, the soldier who had taken human life himself, had his head in his hands, his shoulders shaking. Phyllis was pitched forward, her gaze frozen on the floor. Hugh and Dirk were seething with disbelief and anger, whipsawed by their inability to do anything to save—or, now, avenge—their sister.

The judge sent the case to the jury.

Chapter Eighteen

WHAT REALLY HAPPENED

In the two years since Jayna's death, new information has emerged which shows how close Jayna came to skirting the danger she did not even know existed—Brittany's pathological potential. If events had taken a slightly different turn, Brittany would have been gone and the Lululemon girls would not have been in danger. Jayna did not have to die. For in the days just before she murdered Jayna, Brittany was being watched by the Lulu girls for suspected stealing of their personal possessions and cash. They had her in their sights. As soon as she was caught in the act, Brittany would be on her way out of Lululemon. But when it finally happened, late on a Friday night, Brittany was alone in the store with Jayna.

Two days before Jayna's murder, Brittany's thieving had been the subject of a meeting of the Bethesda leadership team—including Rachel, the manager, plus Jayna, Mikell, Courtney and others. The regular agenda—personnel matters, sales targets—was barely touched. It was all about Brittany.

Some of the Lululemon girls knew that Brittany had been suspected of stealing at the Lululemon in Georgetown. They knew she had been fired from Georgetown for exceeding the staff discount limit on clothing purchases—but then rehired and shifted to Bethesda.

Now they were trying to catch Brittany red-handed. They had mounting evidence that she was purloining cash and personal items from other Lululemon girls. According to one member of the leadership team, Rachel had been told by Lululemon's headquarters that they needed concrete proof to justify dismissal. Because Lululemon had no security cameras, the leadership team even discussed planting a hidden camera. But they were too late. If they had caught Brittany sooner, she would not have had a chance to murder Jayna.

"We knew," said Mikell. "We were aware of things. We just didn't get it in time. That's what's so crappy about it."

On the first Friday evening shift she'd ever worked with Brittany, on a shift that was supposed to include three staffers but was short-handed that night, Jayna caught Brittany shoplifting a pair of yoga pants. Jayna told Brittany that she would have to tell Rachel.

Brittany murdered Jayna.

Based on all that is known, that is almost certainly what really happened. But the jurors, now considering the case in the jury room in November, 2011, knew none of this backstory. Because of the rules banning evidence of unrelated crimes, the jurors knew nothing of the

Brittany Norwood who had demonstrated aberrant tendencies over the last decade of her life. They knew nothing of the young woman's growing trail of deviant behavior, most of it petty, but some of it disturbing. They were ignorant of the court orders—even an arrest warrant—issued against her. They knew nothing of her suspected stealing from Lululemon girls. All this was inadmissible evidence because evidence of crimes or behavior in the past is not considered germane to the crime charged—in this case, murder.

Brittany's shoplifting on the night of the murder, the key precipitating element, was not known to the jury, either. Brittany's shoplifting was known only because Jayna had called Rachel and another Lululemon staffer, Chioma Nwakibu, shortly before she was murdered. Rachel and Chioma had *heard* Jayna *say* that she'd caught Brittany red-handed. That made the phone calls hearsay. Hearsay was not admissible.

* * *

How did Brittany become a thief? How did a young woman with a college education, a strong family, a middle-class upbringing and an exceptional athletic career in a tightly organized sports program turn into a pilferer with the capacity to kill?

According to family, friends and former coaches, Brittany seems to have been a nearly model young person. Brittany's parents stressed hard work and principled living; they supported their kids in school and sports.

"They were very involved, very polite," said a former soccer coach. "I don't know if they ever missed a game." Brittany did well in school. A teacher said Brittany was "an exceptionally talented writer and that she could benefit from this gift"—words that have an eerie ring after the fabulous fiction Brittany concocted.

In personality, Brittany was described as funny, bright, even charismatic. She smiled and laughed a lot. Her photographs, even her last driver's license, show a radiant young woman, in stark contrast to the menacing police mug shot of Brittany that went around the world. Like Jayna, Brittany was described as being concerned for others and particularly good with children. Like Jayna, Brittany had two young nephews that she doted on.

Despite these parallels, Jayna and Brittany turned out, in the end, to be as different as good and evil or, as Jayna's brothers might put it, as heaven and hell. Marisa, Jayna's friend, later said that it did not matter if Brittany had a heart of gold while growing up—as described by her family members—she had become a monster. Jayna's and Brittany's lives followed dramatically different trajectories, Jayna's towards success, Brittany's towards disaster.

Brittany's shaky trajectory began with her move from Seattle to Long Island after high school. When she entered college and became a standout on the Stony Brook Seawolves soccer team, she apparently slipped the bonds of family and constraint that had governed her earlier life. "Something happened," said her lawyer, and "the erosion started." But it was worse than erosion. It was almost as if Brittany developed a dual personality, one a cheerful and caring young woman who wouldn't step on an insect, the other a compulsive liar and pilferer who couldn't restrain her impulses. In biblical terms, argued one of Brittany's aunts, citing the Apostle Paul's first letter to Timothy, Brittany was somehow led astray after leaving home, "giving heed to seducing spirits, and doctrines of devils." (Brittany's mother was also given to citing the Bible.)

The two-faced, devil-seduced Brittany first emerged on the college soccer team. Even while performing impressively as a defensive player at Stony Brook, Brittany was gaining a reputation among her teammates as a thief. Reports of stealing dogged Brittany's college career. One teammate, Leanna Yust, told *The Washington Post* that Brittany was sweet, funny and an "amazing soccer player"—but that "the girl was like a klepto" who stole money and a shirt from her.

Another teammate, Megan Healey, told television reporter McCarren that at first she found Brittany to be "as nice as they come, really friendly, a leader on the team," especially during a trip to Europe for pre-season play. But then other players warned Healey to "watch out for her. ...You might want to keep your stuff close by. She would steal money, she would steal clothing. Clothing was a big thing."

One incident was especially revealing. When a player caught Brittany trying to purloin her purse, Brittany leapt onto the offensive, reversing the narrative. "What are you talking about? You're crazy!" she yelled. She instantly converted herself into the injured party, just as she did 10 years later with a cover-up that cast herself as a co-victim. In a flash, Brittany's dark side had shown.

Brittany attended Stony Brook on an athletic scholarship for four years, where she was a standout soccer star, once named the team's most valuable player and twice named to all-conference teams. But at some point she was kicked off the soccer team for her larcenous behavior, according to prosecutor McCarthy. She never received her college degree—though she told the police she did.

After she moved to Washington, D.C., Brittany became a typically active, well-liked, twenty-something woman about town—while masking a pattern of deviant behavior. Her court record included the relatively mundane transgressions of being sued for failure to pay rent, not appearing in court for failing to pay a speeding ticket, and having a judgment placed against her regarding nearly $20,000 in unpaid student loans. One report, if true, captured her preoccupation with grooming as well as her larceny: A hairdresser blogged that Brittany once ordered expensive imported hair for a full weave, but when it came time to pay, Brittany said the money she'd brought to pay for the services had been stolen from her wallet.

Those delinquencies paled in comparison to a drama that unfolded in 2007 and 2008—and provided the first hint that Brittany might have more than just kleptomaniac tendencies. Brittany broke up with a boyfriend, a Washington dentist whom she had been seeing for about 18 months, after an apparently stormy relationship. The dentist complained in court documents that Brittany "would punch, push and throw things" at him. After they separated, Brittany continued calling and even stalking the dentist and his new girlfriend. She "seems not to understand that the relationship is over," he stated.

Matters came to a head when Brittany invaded the dentist's home—she still had keys and the burglar alarm code. The new girlfriend filed a claim that Brittany stole her possessions from the house: a Movado watch, a Lacoste shirt, Vera Wang perfume, diamond earrings, a cell phone, checks from her check book and her car keys. In her complaint to the D.C. Superior Court Domestic Violence Unit, the new girlfriend said that Brittany had been watching her and the dentist, and that she felt threatened. The dentist said that he feared "for his safety." They filed for a restraining order that required Brittany to stay away from them and to seek counseling for "anger management, psychiatric evaluation."

A temporary restraining order was served on Brittany at the historic Willard InterContinental Hotel, where she was then working. She signed it. But within two weeks she had violated it. The couple saw Brittany watching them from her car in the alley behind the dentist's office. When they left, Brittany followed them to his house then to an Office Depot in Silver Spring,

Maryland. The couple called the police on the spot and filed an additional complaint. Brittany was then ordered to a contempt hearing—which was postponed twice.

Finally, in May 2008, an arrest warrant was issued for Brittany. But it was never carried out. The D.C. Superior Court said that such orders are not executed by the police unless another complaint is filed. An opportunity to confront, expose and sanction Brittany's behavior was lost. Had she been led off to jail for stalking in 2008, would that have deterred her from murdering in 2011?

There was another shocking but murky chapter in Brittany's life that was not admissible at her trial. Based on text messages found in Brittany's cell phone, prosecutors believe she was involved in prostitution, even while she was working at Lululemon. They also discovered a posting on Craigslist offering Brittany's "personal services." Still another suggestive clue appeared when forensics experts at Lululemon picked up two subway farecards from the debris. One was registered to Jayna, the other to a prostitution counseling group. This was a remarkable discovery. Retrieving the farecard in her wallet, which she claimed she left behind at Lululemon, was the reason Brittany had given when persuading Jayna to return to the store that night.

Brittany's stealing, stalking and possible prostitution were presumably not known to Lululemon when Brittany was first hired to work as a sales person at the store in Georgetown. At first, Brittany seemed a good fit. She embodied the qualities of a Lululemon girl: bubbly, friendly and dedicated to the yoga-centric lifestyle of self-improvement.

Within several weeks, however, Brittany was heading for trouble. In addition to being suspected of stealing from the store's cash registers, Brittany made a crucial error at Christmastime. She dramatically exceeded the store's employee discount limit.

Lululemon had a generous employee discount program. The staff could buy clothes at great prices and wear them at work and at workouts. Combined with its policy of offering its employees free passes to local yoga studios and fitness clubs, the clothing deal put the Lululemon girls on display in exactly the right market: upscale women who worked out. Lululemon products are high quality and flattering; other women working out always asked the Lululemon staffers where their outfits came from.

Before Christmas, Lululemon offered its employees even deeper discounts, including a special staff shopping night. But each employee had a purchase ceiling—say $1,000. On this shopping night, Brittany reportedly went far beyond her limit. She was fired.

Brittany was furious. She called her friend Eila to vent. "She poured out her story. She felt she was wrongfully fired. She thought she had her manager's permission to go over the limit," remembered Eila.

Brittany appealed her firing—and won. There was much speculation among Lululemon girls as to why Lululemon hired her back. Exceeding the limit was a widespread practice, they said, but Lululemon was trying to crack down—and made an example of Brittany. It was also speculated that Lululemon may have feared a lawsuit based on racial discrimination.

Over the holidays, Rachel, the manager of the Bethesda store, told her leadership team that Brittany was coming to work at their store. This upset Mikell, who was an assistant manager. She considered it a mistake to bring someone back who might not have the moral character expected in a company "that is all about spirituality."

"I was appalled," says Mikell. "I thought this was messed up. Why hadn't Lululemon just settled with Brittany? I'll never forgive Lululemon for hiring her back."

* * *

Brittany's work at the Bethesda store started off well enough. One week she was featured in the store's weekly email that went out to hundreds of customers. The email was titled, "Want To Be The Hottest In Class? Your Wish Is Our Command." The email included three striking pictures of Brittany modeling a "Hot Class Tank and Bra" with matching pants. Brittany struck several artsy poses, holding a gauzy white bow as an accessory against the all-black outfit. The images were set in a single frame against a light backdrop. Brittany looked like she knew what she was doing. The illustration had a professional sheen. Ironically, it was probably produced by the store's resident computer whiz: Jayna.

But Brittany's presence in the Bethesda store soon turned sour. Several Lululemon girls reported missing possessions, including up to $200 in cash. Even Eila, who was now regularly spending time with Brittany outside of work, began to wonder about Brittany. One day when they had gone to a gym together, Brittany noticed a large bottle of Vera Wang perfume in Eila's workout bag. "Oh, I love that perfume," commented Brittany. It was Eila's favorite, a $70 indulgence. Eila told her to try it out. Later that day, after her shift at Lululemon, Eila discovered that her perfume was missing. Brittany was the last person she had seen using it. She texted Brittany: "Hey, Britt, did I leave my perfume in the store?" Brittany said she had not seen it. Another Lululemon girl later told Eila that she had noticed the perfume in Brittany's bag.

Even Brittany's good friend Nora, who was planning to share an apartment with her in Bethesda, realized one day that $200 was gone from her gym bag. Brittany was the only person who could have taken it. "I called her and asked about it. She just weirdly blew me off," said Nora.

Finally, it was Courtney who discovered cash missing from her bag on Friday, March 4, one week before the murder in the store. The amount was only $10, but even that was striking. "Who would steal 10 dollars?" Courtney wondered. When she reported it to Mikell, the assistant manager replied: "Tell me you're kidding me. You're the third person to report something."

Rachel already suspected Brittany. She had researched the shift schedules and, sure enough, the reports of missing possessions coincided with Brittany's schedule. Yet that was not enough. The Lululemon girls had to get clear proof of Brittany's pilfering to take her down.

The Lulu girls did what they always did when faced with a new challenge: talked incessantly about it. Brittany's stealing dominated the weekly meeting of Rachel's leadership team—five or six staffers, including Jayna, Mikell and Courtney—on Wednesday, March 9, 2011. "We discussed how to catch Brittany in the act. We were calling her 'the thief,'" said Courtney. "We were joking about a nanny cam—putting a camera in a stuffed animal, like on *To Catch a Predator*."

The Lululemon girls were slightly amused to find themselves playing detective. But they were unsure exactly what to do, except keep a watch on Brittany. "From Wednesday on, it was a running conversation about, 'Can we catch her?'" said Courtney. Ironically, she said, they were concerned only with Brittany's theft from her colleagues, not the possibility that she might also be taking things from the store. "We weren't thinking about her stealing clothing at all."

The only decision reached by the leadership was to alert the other employees that "someone in our midst is stealing." The announcement would be made at the next general staff meeting, scheduled for Sunday, four days hence.

In two days, Jayna would be dead.

Chapter Nineteen

FINAL SHIFT

Jayna never worked on Friday nights. But on this Friday, for the first time, she had swapped shifts with Mikell, who wanted to leave early for a weekend at the beach with her boyfriend. It was a happy arrangement for all concerned.

Normally, there were three sales persons on the closing shift, partly for normal staffing purposes, but also as a security measure. After all, the staff was all female. But on this night, of all nights, the third person could not come in and no one had been found to fill her slot. It would be just Jayna and Brittany.

This Friday was a mild pre-spring day in Bethesda, the kind of day that brought out the shoppers. Health-conscious Bethesdans were beginning to eat at the sidewalk tables in front of the Sweet Greens salad bar and Five Guys Burgers along Bethesda Avenue. By that afternoon, they were also lining up for the new Apple iPad 2.

For Brittany, this Friday was a chance to get together with Eila for a pleasant outing before starting her shift at

3 p.m. She and Eila planned a late morning yoga workout together at a new gym called Crunch. Eila was delayed, so Brittany took the class without her. Afterwards they ate lunch at Union Jack's, a British pub in Bethesda known for its thick sandwiches and dark beers. Brittany was in a good mood and had a beer with her food. She talked about her hopes of getting the job at Equinox.

On impulse, Brittany and Eila treated themselves after lunch to a $39 pedicure and manicure at Blue Zen, a small nail spa just down the street from Equinox. Brittany loved having her nails and hair done just right. It was the perfect ending to a midday jaunt by two young women enjoying their friendship, their freedom, the special sisterhood of the Lululemon girls. Brittany had to hurry through the posh arcade of Bethesda Lane, lined with expensive shops like Urban Chic and Le Creuset, to get to work on time. Her nails were still drying when she walked into Lululemon at 3 p.m.

Jayna spent her day trying to catch up on things. After all, Fraser—her boyfriend in Seattle, the man of her life—was flying in the next week for a four-day weekend. They were planning to attend a seminar by Gary Chapman, author of *The 5 Love Languages*. Jayna wanted to have things cleared away, especially her income taxes— her damned taxes! She had already called her friend Rudy Colberg for help. Rudy was the numbers genius, the MBA grad student at the University of Michigan. Jayna was fretting over not paying her fair share of taxes, he remembered. "Turbo Tax was telling her she would get a refund. That bothered her. She didn't think it was right. I told her it was okay and promised to walk her through it over the weekend."

To get some work done on her laptop, Jayna had come in to Lululemon early—around 1 p.m. In the back office, she worked and listened to music on her earbuds. Courtney asked what she was listening to. It was a silly 1950s song called "Lollipop" by The Chordettes. Jayna emailed it to Courtney. Mikell came in and gave Jayna a bottle of red wine to thank her for swapping shifts, then left for the beach. Other Lululemon girls came and went, saying goodbye to Jayna as their shifts neared an end. To cap the day, Courtney and Jayna decided to meet for a drink at Uncle Julio's after Jayna finished work around 9:45 p.m. The Lulu girls often communicated by text, referring to each other by a coded nickname they gave themselves, Jim, or its variations: Jimmy, Jimbo or Jimmers.

Jayna, Mikell and Courtney were conscious of the fraught situation that night: Jayna working alone with Brittany on the closing shift. Jayna joked to Courtney: "I'm closing tonight with the thief. Do you think I'll catch her?"

Courtney laughed: "She's not that dumb!"

Even Mikell texted Jayna: "You're closing with the thief!"

Jayna responded: "Hide your stuff! Ha ha ha!"

Jayna and Brittany had an uneventful evening in the store. Far more people were drawn to the Apple emporium next door because of the iPad 2 release. Even after 9 p.m., Apple's showroom was still buzzing.

Shortly before Lululemon's 9 p.m. closing time, however, Jayna had a major change of plans. Courtney felt she had to cancel their after-work drink. She was tired and had an early shift the next day at another job. She texted Jayna: "I'm exhausted and have to be back at 7. I'm headed home ☹ sorry. Hope you survived!!"

It was a vain hope.

Jayna and Brittany locked Lululemon's front door and began the familiar closing routine, including shutting down the cash registers. As a member of the leadership team, Jayna was half-a-step above Brittany in the store hierarchy. It was her job to lock up.

The night's pivotal drama started shortly before 9:45 p.m., as the two women were preparing to leave. Each woman checked the other's bag for store merchandise. This is routine in the retail world; at Lululemon, it was particularly strict. A staffer had to show her bag before leaving the premises on a break or sandwich run, for example. Since it was common for Lululemon girls to buy Lululemon clothes, it was not uncommon to find items they had purchased in their bags, along with the receipts.

As revealed in phone calls Jayna made before her death, Jayna looked into Brittany's bag and was astonished to find a pair of Lululemon yoga pants with the tags still on.

"Did you buy these?" asked Jayna, stunned. She knew she had probably just caught Brittany in the act of shoplifting.

Brittany had no receipt. She said she'd bought the pants earlier from Chioma, who had worked the day shift. Jayna tried to check the computers for the purchase, but the system was locked down for the night.

Jayna told Brittany they would handle the problem the next day. She also said she would have to tell Rachel about it.

The two women left Lululemon—Jayna to her car, Brittany to the subway. Even before she reached her parking garage, Jayna quickly dialed Chioma's number. Chioma knew all about the effort to catch Brittany. Jayna asked if she had sold Brittany the pants.

"No," replied Chioma. "I can't believe we got her! We did it!"

Jayna then called Rachel, who was in her apartment across from Lululemon. She was packing up for a move.

"We caught the bitch!" Jayna said as soon as Rachel answered.

"We got her!" replied Rachel. She told Jayna not to worry about it anymore. She was going to fire Brittany the next day. It looked like a quick and easy resolution to the Brittany problem.

As she was driving towards Virginia, however, Jayna's phone rang. To her surprise, it was Brittany. Brittany said she was sorry but she'd left her wallet in the store and needed to go back. Could Jayna come back and let her in?

Jayna said it was okay. She'd forgotten her laptop, too. She turned around and drove back to Lululemon. She tried calling Rachel again to tell her what was happening. But she got no answer.

By the time Brittany returned to Lululemon, she had had 20 minutes to stew over what had happened in the store. Jayna had caught her with unpaid-for yoga pants worth nearly $100. Brittany knew Jayna was going to tell Rachel. Brittany had already been fired once from Lululemon. If she were fired again, her chances of getting the job as a personal trainer at the Equinox gym were down the drain. Her new career path would be ended before it started.

At 10:05 p.m., Jayna opened Lululemon's front door and hit the buttons to kill the alarm. At 10:10 p.m., Apple Store managers began hearing strange noises through the wall. At 10:19 p.m., they walked away from the wall. The noises were becoming quieter. Soon they were silent.

Jayna Murray lay motionless in the back hallway and Brittany Norwood was thinking about how to deceive the world.

Chapter Twenty

THE VERDICT

McCarthy and Ayres feared the jury might not find Brittany guilty of first-degree murder for one primary reason: They had no truly convincing motive. They could not present the most compelling trigger for the attack—Jayna's discovery of Brittany's shoplifting and Jayna's statement that she would have to inform Rachel, the Lululemon manager. They could not introduce the Lululemon girls' efforts to try to catch Brittany in the act or Jayna's phone calls to Chioma and Rachel. "Lack of motive shows it was someone who lost control," said Brittany's attorney, arguing for a second-degree conviction.

McCarthy and Ayres were left with the testimony of the Apple Store staffers. "Talk to me! Tell me what's going on!" shouted Brittany, as the Apple employees heard it. Ayres argued that Brittany was furious at Jayna for refusing to discuss further her plans to tell Rachel about the theft. Jayna was, effectively, ignoring Brittany. "If you want to get at someone, you ignore them when they want to talk to you," reasoned Ayres. "One of the most irritating things for human beings is when you want to talk to someone and they are shutting you down."

Ayres told the jury: "The implication is, 'Tell me what's going on or I'll kill you,' That is the reason she killed her."

Ayres also contended that Brittany was planning to attack Jayna from the moment she lured her back to the store with the false claim that she had forgotten her wallet. "This was a lure and a sneak attack," said Ayres. "Jayna fell for the dupe." (Brittany, on the other hand, had told her brother that "I really did forget my wallet.")

The prosecutors need not have worried. The absence of a clear motive was no impediment to the jury's decision. While some jurors were bothered by the lack of a convincing motive, their reservations were overcome by the sheer brutality and duration of the attack. "Brittany lost it," said juror Donny Knepper. "But she had to have cognition when she decided to puncture the [victim's] brain stem. On the jury, there was no real deliberation. We were all convinced."

Within minutes, the jurors had voted on whether to convict: All twelve hands went up. Brittany Norwood was guilty of premeditated first-degree murder. The trial was effectively over.

Cheers and applause rose from Jayna's family and friends when the foreman said the word: *Guilty*. Justice, the Murrays felt, had been done—at least as much as could be done without bringing Jayna back to life. "It was the greatest that I've ever felt in my life," David Murray said that night on television. The Norwood family left the courthouse without a word to the media, maintaining the silence they had kept throughout the trial.

After the guilty verdict, only one issue remained: Would Brittany get life in prison *with* the possibility of parole, or life in prison *without* the possibility of parole. That question would be answered three months later, once Judge Greenberg considered the case and received victim impact statements from the two families and their friends.

The sentencing in January 2012 was high drama. Six members of Jayna's family and several of her friends took the stand to make moving, detailed statements about Jayna's life and their own sense of loss.

In a six-page, single-spaced essay that took 27 minutes to deliver, David outlined Jayna's three high-wire decades on Earth and spoke of the "indefinable nightmare" that his life had become since her murder. Phyllis Murray quoted from a school worksheet Jayna had written at age 10, calling herself a "laughy person" who disliked "people who are not honest and that try to hurt others." Jayna's brother, Hugh, declared himself "a victim of murder" and reminded everyone that "Jayna went back [to Lululemon] to help Brittany Norwood." Jayna's other brother, Dirk, a commercial pilot, said that since his sister's murder, he had been reading two books: the Bible and Dante's *Inferno*. Hell, Dante noted, "is reserved for the real hard cases," and it is this inferno that awaits Brittany. Kate Murray, Hugh's wife, asked Judge Greenberg to "finish what Jayna started" when she exposed Brittany for shoplifting—put her behind bars forever. April Murray, Dirk's wife, said that Brittany's only contributions to society had been "lies and sickness, like cancer," and that she should have to give the rest of her life as repayment.

Fraser Bocell and Marisa Connaughton also testified.

The statements echoed through the courtroom for nearly two hours.

Brittany's family responded with a series of written statements. But only one was delivered in the courtroom: that of her oldest brother, Sandré Norwood. He said that Brittany was a "good person" who would always carry the shame and dishonor of having been "convicted of a horrific crime." Sandré asked for leniency for Brittany. His statement lasted seven minutes.

The biggest question in everyone's mind that cold January day was whether Brittany herself would speak. Wavering until the last moment, she finally decided to break her silence when Judge Greenberg asked if she wanted to say anything. Her voice cracking, she apologized to the Murrays "for the crime I've been convicted of." Acknowledging that nothing she said could assuage the pain "when your daughter's gone and I am the one who has been convicted of her murder," she nonetheless needed to tell them "just how deeply sorry I am." With others in the courtroom openly sobbing, Brittany told her family that she "couldn't have asked for a better one." Finally, she asked the judge to leave her with "some hope"—an appeal for a life sentence that included the possibility of parole someday.

Brittany got her answer immediately. Denouncing the "barbaric nature" of her crime, Judge Robert Greenberg, who had run a meticulously proper trial, said that he saw almost no chance of Brittany's ever being rehabilitated. Her acts, he said, represented "the worst of human behavior." She had plenty of opportunities to stop her brutality, but did not take them. "After every blow, you had a chance to think about what you were doing," said Greenberg. Instead, "you mutilated this woman." He sentenced Brittany to spend the rest of her days incarcerated, no matter what—life imprisonment without the possibility of parole. Brittany would die behind bars.

In addition, the judge went out of his way to criticize the Apple Store staffers. Speaking for the Murray family's outrage—and the Bethesda community's incredulity—he blasted "the callous indifference of the people who worked at the Apple Store who heard this [crime] happen and did not a blessed thing to stop it." His words were a fitting coda to the scorching of the Apple employees in the local media and the blogosphere. (Greenberg's opprobrium extended to Apple, the parent company, as well. Representatives of the consumer electronics giant never reached out to the Murray family, never made the slightest gesture of regret or compassion, never even issued a statement on the case. "'Apple refused to comment,' is fine," said a corporate spokesman in Cupertino, California, when called two years after the murder.)

The sad drama of the murder in the yoga store had reached its finale. Jayna was buried in the ground and Brittany was now buried in a state prison for life. For Jayna's family, for the prosecution, for the once-terrorized Bethesda community, it was a fitting end. Justice had been served. But it was not a satisfying end. Everyone was left with the looming question: Why?

Chapter Twenty-One

WHY?

Nobody could believe that getting caught while shoplifting a $98 pair of pants could account for murder, especially a murder like this. There had to be another explanation.

"*Why*? That's my question, still..." said David Murray, Jayna's father, when I first met him in Texas. Even 18 months after his daughter's murder, after the long and excruciating trial, after the verdict and sentence that he and his family wanted, a mourning man with a gaping hole in his heart knows there is a gnawing mystery that may never be solved. Unless Brittany tells it—and who would believe her even if she did?—her motive and mood, her reasoning and lack of it, her precise actions and decisions may never be known.

So far, Brittany has not publicly addressed these questions, and did not respond to my request for an interview. But there was no lack of public speculation.

As I listened to the chatter at Quartermaine Coffee Roasters on Bethesda Avenue or at the Barnes

& Noble café on the corner, I could hear all the theories. Some people figured embezzlement must have been involved. Others gravitated to tabloid tales, the usual variations on sexual themes. There must have been a lesbian connection, a secret love affair gone wrong. Or maybe a love triangle that set Jayna and Brittany at one another's throats—Brittany was from Seattle and Fraser, Jayna's expected future husband, was in Seattle studying for his doctorate.

Besides sex, there was race. Was Brittany's eruption of violence a sudden release of pent-up racial rage and class resentments? After all, Jayna was "the golden girl with the perfect family and the perfect life," said one observer, while Brittany, though middle-class, was still struggling to find her footing.

Nothing in the somewhat sparse record of Brittany's life supports any of these theories. Knowledgeable observers dismiss the sexual scenarios out of hand. And none of the Murrays or any of the Lululemon girls I talked to believed Brittany bore any particular racial grudge. Outwardly, at least, Brittany's love of the good life, her easy assimilation into the comforts and privileges of Bethesda, suggest that she was barely race-conscious herself. "She was the whitest African American I've ever known," said one Lululemon girl.

This leaves psychopathy. Brittany's quantum leap from "from stealing $10 to murder in six days," as Courtney put it, shifts the discussion into the realm of the psychologically unhinged. The extreme brutality of Brittany's acts invites comparisons with Hannibal Lecter, the fictional psychiatrist in *The Silence of the Lambs.* Lecter was Detective Ruvin's instant frame of reference. The psychopathic theme, with all its extremes, is so compelling and popular that NBC brought Hannibal back, with new and grisly twists, as a fresh television series in spring 2013.

A psychopath is the perfect villain. The psychopath is scarier than other criminals, even murderers, because his (or her) behavior cannot be explained within the usual categories that drive aberrant behavior—greed, lust, hate, rage. The psychopath has a more fundamental failing than a momentary loss of control—she has a permanent personality flaw or mental disorder often called an antisocial personality disorder. In popular usage, the psychopath kills for "no reason." Or at least we cannot figure out the reason. As far as most of us are concerned, a psychopath is crazy.

But psychopathy is, in some ways, an attempt to explain insane behavior by a person who is not insane. Brittany, despite some hopes by her attorney to prove otherwise, had no provable mental disease. She could not be shown to be insane. Even her brother knew that. But she had acted crazy.

In the scientific literature, a psychopath or a sociopath—a variation on the type—has no conscience. She cannot feel empathy. She does not sense remorse.

Her emotions are shallow and she acts impulsively. She can be grandiose, manipulative, consistently irresponsible and have poor behavior controls. Yet she can be glib and have a kind of "sociopathic charisma."

These characteristics are laid out in several key books. One is *Without Conscience: The Disturbing World of Psychopaths Among Us*, published in 1993 by Robert D. Hare, a professor in British Columbia. The book contains a widely used "Psychopathy Checklist" that Hare developed four decades ago while studying prison inmates and others. Another primary source is the *Diagnostic and Statistical Manual of Mental Disorders*, the bible of psychiatric labeling. The book's fifth edition, known as DSM 5, was published in May 2013, to great controversy.

Finally, there is *The Sociopath Next Door: The Ruthless Versus the Rest of Us*, a book written in 2005 by psychologist Martha Stout. Stout's book became a persuasive explainer of Brittany's behavior to some of the people most affected by Jayna's murder. Marybeth Ayres, the assistant state's attorney, believes that Brittany was a "textbook example" of a sociopath. She believes Brittany's history of deviant behavior— stealing, stalking, maybe prostituting—shows a lack of conscience and empathy, which made it possible for Brittany to murder Jayna, and to do it viciously. Detective Ruvin shares her view.

Ayres recommended the book to Jayna's family, the Murrays. They found it convincing. To them,

Brittany belongs to what Stout says is a 4 percent segment of the U.S. population that is sociopathic. They found Brittany's demeanor in court—always staring blankly ahead or down, never betraying emotion—as evidence of her lack of empathy, conscience or remorse.

Because Brittany's act was otherwise baffling, the sociopathic analysis is appealing and makes a certain amount of sense. Surely her lethal explosion was unexplainable on the "normal" scale of criminal behavior—for money, for love, for revenge, even for escape from the tight spot she had gotten into by shoplifting. But most of the typologies presented by the experts were developed to better understand people with long histories of violence, people already doing long prison terms. In many cases they were serial killers, like Edward Gein, the cannibalistic murderer on whom characters in *The Silence of the Lambs* are partially based.

Brittany's murder was a singular act. She had never done anything like it before, had no public record of serious violence—besides the pushing and shoving with her former boyfriend, the dentist. As far as is known, she had no childhood history of torturing animals or starting fires, classic early symptoms of antisocial tendencies. Yet she had no compunctions about stealing from those around her, even from friends like Eila and Nora. Conscienceless pilfering, without remorse, certainly fits a prime definition of sociopathy.

Something extraordinary happened that puts Brittany outside the pale of normal behavior, even beyond the bounds of most criminal behavior. She committed what most of us would call a psychopathic act, our shorthand for crazy, deranged, unexplainable. And that is the dilemma. The human head and heart want logic and explanations. We want the pieces—even the ugly ones—to fit together. Brittany's pieces are not fitting. And, unless Brittany someday decides to shed light on herself and her horrific acts, the world may have to live with that. Unsatisfying as it is, the lingering question surrounding the Lululemon store murder will remain: "Why?"

EPILOGUE

In the end, the Murray family and Jayna's legion of friends took comfort from knowing that it was Jayna's sojourn on the planet that made a mark, not Brittany's. As Brittany faded into oblivion, an ugly footnote to history, Jayna's spirit—do it now, try whatever scares you, treasure your family and friends—thrived in their memories, in their lives, even in their pain. After dozens of interviews, after hours and hours of conversation with those who knew her best, I was astonished repeatedly to hear stories of Jayna's uplifting impact on those around her. People talked about Jayna with a certain awe and admiration, and talked of changing their lives to be more like hers.

"Her words were like the Bible to me," said Mikell. "Because of Jayna, I decided never to put off anything I intended to do in life," said Matt. Patrick said Jayna taught him how to focus on others. Courtney said "I loved that woman" and got a tattoo on her arm in Jayna's memory.

For some, the anguish lingered. More than a year after Jayna's death, Leah decided to give up her job and take a close-to-the-Earth journey around the world with her husband, hoping to heal. Marisa bitterly missed Jayna's laugh and spirit at her own bachelorette party just before her wedding—"it wasn't the same without Jayna." Cynthia, whose wedding Jayna was in, cannot say the words "Jayna died" without beginning to cry.

Jayna's family decided to celebrate her life rather than dwell on her death. Hugh and Dirk set up a foundation in Jayna's name to fund scholarships at her former schools and camps. David Murray wears a metal medallion around his neck bearing Jayna's standard signature—"Jayna XOXO"—"and I will never take it off," he says. Phyllis, Jayna's mother, carries the same thing on her purse. Jayna's yoga pose photo hangs in Lululemon's Bethesda store, which rebuilt its façade with a stained glass fanlight reading "Love" in honor of Jayna. Finally, Jayna's adventurous spirit is online for all to see in her YouTube video, "Learning To Fly on my 30th Birthday."

The big smile lives.

ACKNOWLEDGEMENTS

My heartfelt compassion and deepest thanks go to Jayna Murray's family: Phyllis, David, Kate, Hugh, Dirk and April. While continuing to endure incomprehensible pain that is the worst nightmare of every parent and sibling, they gave generously of their time and hearts, sharing a lifetime of memories and significant moments about their daughter and sister. Their words brought to life Jayna's intensity, vitality and joyous personality better than anything I could ever write; I am grateful for their willingness to tell Jayna's story. They are a remarkable family.

Special thanks also go to Montgomery County state's attorneys John McCarthy and Marybeth Ayres who played the crucial role in obtaining a maximum verdict and maximum sentence—and in reconstructing the story. They were central to unraveling the complexities of the case.

Likewise I am indebted to Montgomery County Detectives Dimitry Ruvin and Jim Drewry, who deserve credit, along with their many colleagues, for solving the crime—and also for helping to tell the tale. In addition, I was assisted by Sergeant Craig Wittenberger and Assistant Chief Russell Hamill.

Other members of the vast Jayna Murray family of friends and colleagues were extremely important and gave me sometimes grief-racked stories from Jayna's life:

Courtney Kelly, Mikell Belser, Marisa Connaughton, Leah McFail, Melissa Jersey, Gena've Ramirez, Cynthia Isaacson, Eila Rab, Patrick Byrnett, Matt Deschner, Rudy Colberg, Heather Barron, Judd Borakove, Laura Timms and Cecy Zimmerman.

A number of Jayna's friends and former colleagues at Halliburton met with me in Houston: Myron Malek, Sheila R. Le Blanc and Steve Matthews. I also had good conversations with Jayna's most important dance teacher, Michelle Smith, and an early track coach, Andy Stewart.

I'm grateful also for discussions with Nora Mann, a personal trainer, and Scott Rosen, chief operating officer of the Equinox, the luxury gym chain.

My thanks go to the many public servants who responded expertly and helpfully to my many requests: Linda Daly, Greg Hilton, Brian Saccenti, Ramon Korionoff and Dave Seeman.

Some key players in Bethesda and Montgomery County gave of their time, too—including Roger Berliner, Dave Dabney, Dave Feldman, Seth Goldman and Chris Palmer. Special thanks to Matt Touhey and Margarita Lisi.

A writer is always indebted to professional colleagues. These include Andrea McCarren of WUSA-TV and Neal Augenstein of WTOP radio in Washington, D.C. Maureen O'Hagan of the *Seattle Times* did research in Brittany Norwood's home town. Brian vanBlommestein talked to me about Norwood's soccer career.

I owe a special debt of gratitude to my close circle of friends and colleagues who were willing readers, outstanding editors and indispensible supporters during the writing of this book. The first among them is Laurence Latourette, whose strangely sharp insights, brutal honesty and fair judgments were of critical help. His friendship is inestimable. Thanks go as well to Rollie Flynn.

LeeAnn Jackson played a crucial role, bringing a clear editor's eye and sense of narrative to the finishing process as she repeatedly copy-edited the manuscript.

My first readers also included a unique crew who are near and dear to me. First and foremost in this group is Caroline Harkleroad, my sister and a longtime publishing professional with a laser-like instinct for a good story well told. I also received valuable inputs from five other important women in my life: Julie Range, Laura Post, Jen Lim, Carrie White and Jill Greene. Their enthusiasm was infectious.

My son, Shannon Range, was the book's web creator and a light of family devotion. My son, Chris Range, was a touchstone of common sense and courage.

A special nod to valued writer friends who were there for me in ways only writers understand: Bruce Kluger, Laurence Leamer, Roger M. Williams, Dan E. Moldea, Gus Russo, Jonetta Rose Barras and Arthur Jay Harris.

No book happens without first-rate editors. I was blessed to have Dave Blum, Andrew Eisenman and

Simone Gorrindo as the good shepherds of this book at Amazon's Kindle Singles publishing arm. I also had the talents and support of *Bethesda Magazine* editors Steve Hull and Lisa Shroder.

For all that help, however, nobody contributed more to the success of this project than my wife and true love, Linda M. Harris. Not only was she my steadfast supporter and constant mood-booster, but she was the best editor this book had. She understood from the beginning the power of the story in its simplest form, and constantly brought me back from writerly wanderings to the essentials. She added invaluable ideas and insights; she always led from the heart. There are no words.

And, with a hug, special thanks to Zachary Range, my youngest son, who kept me grounded throughout the many months of this project. He was a constant reminder of what is truly important in life.

A NOTE ON SOURCES

Murder In The Yoga Store is a dramatic narrative of a true story. It is based on 2,888 pages of trial and pre-trial transcript; on the full-length, six-day audio recording of the trial (it took me two weeks to listen to it and take notes on it); on secret police videos of conversations with Brittany Norwood; on numerous news accounts; on examinations of all the physical and written evidence stored in about ten boxes in two different courthouses— including material that was not used in the trial.

Just as important, this story is result of more than four dozen extensive interviews, including many hours with the generous Murray family, the prosecutors, the police, Jayna's friends and many other sources.

The book was also based on my personal experience as a Washington, D. C., citizen who is constantly in Bethesda, Maryland. I was in front of the Lululemon store on the morning that the murderous attack was discovered. The events in this narrative occurred practically on my doorstep. I had to write the story.

Made in the USA
Lexington, KY
09 January 2015